CW00927471

HEDGEHOGS

HEDGEHOGS
• PAT MORRIS •

With illustrations by
GUY TROUGHTON

Whittet Books

First published 1983
Reprinted 1983, 1984, 1985, 1987
Text © 1983 by Pat Morris
Illustrations © 1983 by Guy Troughton
Whittet Books Ltd, The Oil Mills, Weybridge, Surrey

Design by Jacque Solomons
All rights reserved

British Library Cataloguing in Publication Data

Morris, Pat
  Hedgehogs
  1. Hedgehogs
  I. Title   II. Troughton, Guy
  599.3'3   QL737.153

ISBN 0–905483–28–6

Poem 'Requiem for a Hedgehog', p.87, reprinted by kind permission of Avon Wildlife.

Printed in Great Britain at the University Printing House, Oxford

Contents

Preface

Everyone has a soft spot for the hedgehog. It is one of the most instantly recognized animals and yet one of the most poorly studied British mammals. Many people put out food for their hedgehogs and want to know more about these intriguing creatures, yet there are few books that one can turn to for information.

The present book is intended to provide simple, but factual and down-to-earth information in sufficient quantity and detail to be useful but not overwhelming. The book is suitable to be read all at once or dipped into as and when interest or need dictates. It's meant to reflect the fun and interest of hedgehogs; it's not a dry textbook.

Many people will have their own observations and hedgehog stories; many will feel that a lot has been left out, but this is intended to be a comprehensive book without being expensive. It's not an encyclopædia. There is indeed much more to be said. There is also a lot more to be learned and it is often dangerous to generalize, especially about hedgehogs, based on only a few observations.

When more studies have been done in more different places we will be in a stronger position to give definitive answers to questions about the Natural History of the Hedgehog. In the meanwhile, here is an interim statement; I hope you find it interesting, informative and enjoyable.

Royal Holloway College, University of London   *Dr Pat Morris*, 1982

This book seen and approved by hedgehogs

Acknowledgments

Countless people have contributed in small ways to my knowledge of hedgehogs and to maintaining my interest in them and much of the information contained in this book has been gleaned from the research reports of other biologists in Britain and abroad. My students Nigel Reeve, Andy Wroot, Simone Bullion, Warren Cresswell and Richard Leishman have collectively devoted thousands of hours to investigating aspects of hedgehog biology, in the dark, in fog and rain in order to answer my questions about what hedgehogs get up to. I am especially grateful to them for their fortitude and for what they have spared me having to do for myself. I am also grateful to Mr and Mrs R. Wall for letting us intrude into their garden, interfere with their hedgehogs and generally make a nuisance of ourselves in the dead of night for more than five years. The kind and unstinting co-operation of the authorities responsible for a Royal Park and a West London golf course has provided us with ideal study sites for what remain the only major field investigations of hedgehog ecology in Britain. Similarly I owe much to certain gamekeepers for saving dead hedgehogs for me and to long-suffering friends like Dr Derek Yalden for undertaking studies of bits of hedgehog thus obtained. I am also grateful to my mother for typing the text of this book and before that the two PhD theses and a score or more papers and magazine articles from which the book has drawn extensively.

Some of my studies on hedgehogs have been aided by funds from the Universities Federation for Animal Welfare, the People's Trust for Endangered Species, the Mammal Society and several generous individuals. The Hedgehog Preservation Society has also been very helpful in providing financial support for further hedgehog studies and I am grateful to all.

What's in a name?

The name 'hedgehog' is definitely of English origin, but seems to have come into use about 1450. The old Anglo Saxon name was *il*, evidently derived from the German word *igel*, still used there today.

Country folk often call the hedgehog 'urchin', a word which seems to be derived from Norman French. In the recent past there have been many other country names used for the hedgehog in various areas, 'hedgepig' and 'furzepig' being perhaps the best known. Few of these are in use today. The animal also has its own name in Gaelic (which is the rather uncomplimentary *gráinéog* meaning 'horrible one'), in Welsh and old Cornish.

The Latin word for hedgehog is *Erinaceus* and was chosen in 1758 by the Swedish naturalist Linnaeus to be henceforth the scientific name by which the hedgehog and its kin would be known throughout the world in the classification of the Animal Kingdom.

Hedgehogs pop up in the writings of William Shakespeare in *The Tempest* and *Midsummer Night's Dream*; elsewhere he calls them 'hedgepigs' and 'urchins' but at least we know what he was talking about. Citations in the Bible are more problematical and Biblical scholars have argued at length about the hedgehog's inclusion in the scriptures. The difficulty seems to be due to ambiguity in translations. The Hebrew word *kippod* is rendered as 'hedgehog' in some English versions of the Bible and 'bittern' in others. The difference could hardly be greater and there seems to be no way of sorting out just what is really meant. The only certainty is that there are indeed hedgehogs (and bitterns!) to be found in the Holy Land and so they could quite properly be called Biblical animals and must have been familiar to Biblical people.

Evolution: the hedgehog's pedigree and family history

Skinhog

Our modern hedgehogs have no really close relatives among other mammals. They have distant links with moles, shrews and certain foreign animals which are grouped together and called 'the Insectivora'. This is a bit misleading because many of them feed on things other than insects and they are often very dissimilar in appearance.

In fact hedgehogs are a family all on their own. The modern forms simply evolved from more ancient ones and have been a separate evolutionary line for millions of years. The first hedgehogs probably appeared over 15 million years ago, long before sabre-toothed tigers, woolly rhinos, mammoths and other modern upstarts. Those creatures are now extinct, but the hedgehog is with us still. It's as though the Mark 1 hedgehog was sufficiently well adapted to its way of life that nothing better has yet evolved to replace it. There have been a few evolutionary experiments, like a pig-sized Mediterranean hedgehog; but they didn't work and the various species of modern hedgehogs are all about the same size and shape as our own.

Just because our hedgehog has been around for a long time, it doesn't mean that it has always been found in Britain. During the past million years there have been several major ice ages, during which the hedgehog must have retreated to the warmer parts of the Continent, then re-invaded when the climate improved. This was no problem to a land animal so long as we retained a land connection with

Europe. This was only lost when rising sea levels, caused by melting ice at the end of the last glaciation, finally isolated Britain as an island about 7,000 years ago. By then hedgehogs were well established here, along with Stone Age Man and his successors.

Because the hedgehog has such an ancient lineage and has had so little reason to change, it retains many primitive features that were probably characteristic of the very first mammals of all. The teeth, feet and skeleton for example are all very basic. The senses and brain, centred on smell rather than vision, are similarly very primitive though no less useful for all that.

Similarity is only skin-deep

The most obvious characteristic of the hedgehog is its spiny coat. This leads people, not unreasonably, to the assumption that hedgehogs are closely related to other conspicuously spiny animals such as porcupines. But jumping to such a simple conclusion is like saying that a judge is similar to a beauty queen because both appear to have long curly hair— appearances can be deceptive! In fact porcupines are rodents (like rats, squirrels and guinea pigs) with fundamental differences between them and hedgehogs. There are other spiny rodents (spiny rats from S. America and spiny mice from Africa) as well as

Australian spiny anteaters and some spiny Madagascan things called tenrecs. But all of these have evolved spines quite independently. Their spines, like the hedgehog's, are specially modified hairs; but in none of them are the spines so elaborate.

When fundamentally dissimilar creatures evolve a similar structure and begin superficially to resemble each other, biologists refer to the phenomenon as 'convergent evolution'. The copy-cat evolution of spines in hedgehogs and all these other animals is a good example of this.

Echidna or spiny anteater

Porcupine

Spiny mouse of Africa

Tenrec

Hedgehog species

The hedgehogs form a distinctive family of about a dozen or so species. These include five kinds of hairy hedgehogs or 'moon rats' which live in S.E. Asia and don't have any spines. The different species of typical spiny hedgehogs look very similar and differ from our British one in relatively minor respects (e.g. in having black and white spines, longer ears or white belly fur). There are three species in Africa, a couple in China and the long-eared hedgehog found in the deserts of the Middle East and India.

'Our' hedgehog was also introduced from Britain to New Zealand at the turn of the century by homesick settlers anxious to make their new country as familiar as the old homeland. Hedgehogs are now doing very nicely there. They have become very widespread and abundant on both islands. Hedgehogs have not been introduced successfully to any other distant places; there are no hedgehogs in North or South America, nor in Australia.

Our own British hedgehog, scientifically known as *Erinaceus europaeus*, is the same species that occurs throughout most of the Continent. In eastern Europe and across into Russia, the local hedgehogs typically are bigger than ours and have a white chest. This and some other minor features have tempted biologists to consider these animals to be a different species from ours.

Throughout Europe, hedgehogs are found in farmland, forest and fragmented suburban habitats. They live up mountains, at least to the tree line, but don't care for wet places like marshes. In very dry areas, especially in some of the Mediterranean countries, another species (the North African one) is found. In the north, hedgehogs occur up to about 60°N. latitude; approximately the limit of deciduous trees across southern Scandinavia and Finland.

The hedgehog in Britain

In Britain, the hedgehog is one of our more widely distributed species. It is found almost everywhere, but tends to be scarce or absent from wet areas and it also seems not to like extensive pine forests. Upland habitats such as moorland and mountainsides are not very popular either, probably because they lack both suitable food and suitable nesting places.

Unlike the mole, the common shrew and some other British mammals, the hedgehog does occur in Ireland and is quite common there. Hedgehogs are also found on various Scottish islands, posing the question of how they got there. These islands have not been linked to the mainland since before the last Ice Age, and so their hedgehogs could not have arrived on foot. Nor are they likely to have swum to places like Orkney and Shetland (or to other islands such as Jersey or the Isles of Wight or Man). Their presence must be due to introductions by humans. You might think that nobody would bother taking hedgehogs by boat to such places (though people get very attached to their pet hedgehogs); but this animal is likely to be carted about accidentally. It normally hides away in the daytime (and over winter), often choosing such places as hay or brushwood piles for concealment. It would be very easy indeed to scoop up a heap of peat 'turves' or thatching material, complete with hedgehog inside, and carry it away 'over the sea to Skye'. Many of the Scottish islands lack fuel, building materials and animal fodder; so regular forays to the mainland have probably been quite normal for perhaps thousands of years. The accidental importation of hedgehogs and other animals is not only explicable but almost inevitable.

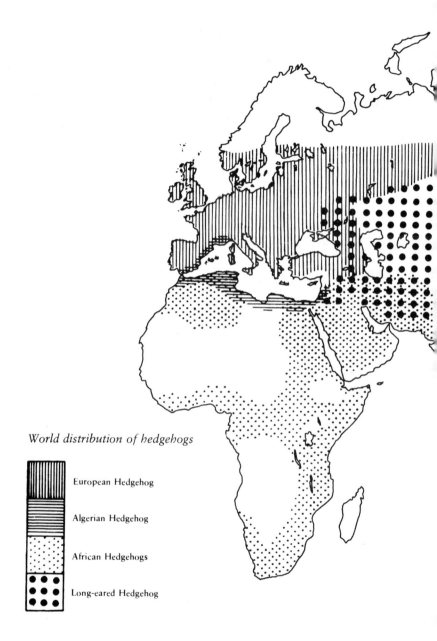

World distribution of hedgehogs

	European Hedgehog
	Algerian Hedgehog
	African Hedgehogs
	Long-eared Hedgehog

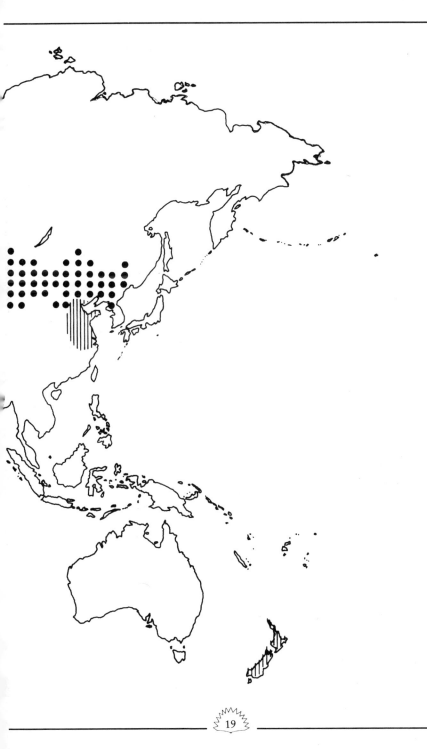

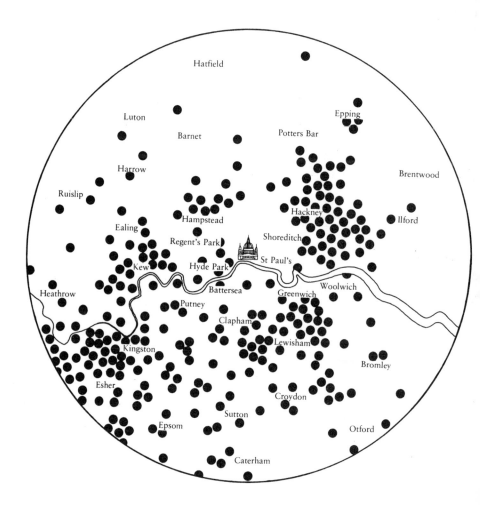

Hatfield

Luton

Barnet

Epping

Potters Bar

Harrow

Brentwood

Ruislip

Hampstead

Hackney

Ilford

Ealing

Regent's Park

Shoreditch

St Paul's

Kew

Hyde Park

Heathrow

Battersea

Woolwich

Greenwich

Putney

Clapham

Kingston

Lewisham

Bromley

Esher

Croydon

Epsom

Sutton

Otford

Caterham

Hedgehogs are common in London, even in the inner suburbs. This map shows a twenty-mile circle round St Paul's indicating areas in which hedgehogs have been recorded in the past thirty years. They are <u>probably common</u> in most blank areas too, except possibly in the very centre.

A notable feature of the hedgehog's distribution in Britain is its abundance in urban and suburban habitats. In the London area, for example, hedgehogs are found well into the inner suburbs (e.g. Willesden, Hampstead, West Ham, Deptford, Streatham, Wimbledon) and there are substantial permanent populations in some of the central London parks (e.g. Holland Park and Regent's Park). Presumably it was a member of the St James's Park population who was reported by *The Times* to have been caught exploring the Admiralty in Whitehall!

The abundance of suburban hedgehogs is not only a pleasure to the people who live there, but also a source of optimism about the future. We tend to contemplate gloomily the expansion of urban sprawl into the countryside, assuming that this cancerous growth automatically obliterates all wildlife. Whereas this may indeed be a serious threat to some animals, it is clear that the hedgehog is not bothered by the spread of bricks and mortar. Indeed the complex of parks, gardens, cemeteries, railway land and waste ground is much to its liking — especially as the human inhabitants of the houses insist on putting out masses of free food. Admittedly some of this is actually intended for pets and for birds; but it's good stuff for hedgehogs too and a shame to see it wasted on overfed cats. The features that make surburbia inconvenient for many animals (disturbance, garden fences, lack of hiding places, etc.) are certainly not a problem for hedgehogs who prosper and multiply.

It may be assumed that many suburban gardens are too small to support hedgehogs. But remember that although *we* may feel confined by fences and garden hedges, hedgehogs are not. A tiny 30ft. × 20ft. garden is indeed too small to support a hedgehog, but if it backs on to another garden and has a row either side the total area available to hedgehogs may be quite considerable. If a garden is entirely walled in or surrounded by a totally impermeable fence, then hedgehogs will have to give it a miss but few fences lack holes of some sort and a hedgehog's nightly wanderings will often be governed by where the gates and fence holes are. Indeed they may forage along a road verge or field edge, making separate excursions into each garden as they pass the gate.

Any animal that can come to terms with surburbia, our one major expanding habitat, has a great advantage over the many species which suffer so much these days from habitat destruction. The hedgehog's success in and around towns is not just a pleasant surprise, but surely a valuable safeguard and insurance for its future survival.

The hedgehog's body: from the outside

There's no mistaking a hedgehog for anything else. It's our only spiny mammal. This particular feature and the persuasive resemblance to a clockwork toy mean that we instantly recognize a hedgehog for what it is and do not closely inspect the details of its anatomy. For example, have you ever noticed a hedgehog's tail? Are you sure it's got one? In fact there is a tail about $\frac{3}{4}''$ (2 cm) long.

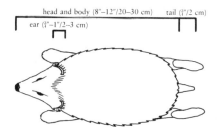

head and body (8″–12″/20–30 cm)   tail (¾″/2 cm)

ear (¾″–1″/2–3 cm)

You don't normally see a hedgehog's legs and feet either, so that when it's walking slowly it seems to be trundling along on wheels. Actually the legs are quite long, 4″ (10 cm) from hip to toe, but normally hidden under a 'skirt' formed by the long hairs at the edge of the spiny part of the skin along the flanks. The voluminous, loose skin acts almost like a bell tent, or a nun's habit, hiding all that's underneath, especially when the hedgehog is 'slumped down', so to speak. If it wants to move fast, it can raise itself up, extend its legs and show a clean pair of heels – literally (see p. 23). As it walks off the heels are visible from the rear. The hind feet are $1\frac{1}{4}''$ (3–4 cm) long and rather narrow. The front feet are shorter but usually broader, so the two leave distinctly different footprints on mud or clean surfaces (the tracks seem to be made by *two* animals, but they aren't – just front and back of the same one).

Powerful forefoot and claws for digging

Fore

Hind

Footprints

The hedgehog's vital statistics change somewhat with age, just as they do in humans: old hedgehogs often tend to be big and fat; and males tend to be bigger than females. Body weight is one of the hedgehog's most variable features but also one of the most helpful in giving us clues about age and health. One-year-old hedgehogs usually weigh about 1 lb–1½ lb (450–680 g); heavier ones are normally older. However, weight varies greatly with the seasons – a one-year-old animal may double its weight in the course of its second summer as it lays down fat for hibernation. Body weight is very much governed by abundance of food. Early in the year, when fat reserves are exhausted and there is little natural food to be found, some adults may weigh only 12 oz (350 g) (like a 6-stone man) and are badly in need of food. When well fed, British hedgehogs can grow to a weight of 2½ lb (1,200 g) or more in the wild, but pet hedgehogs with indulgent owners can just grow and grow. The biggest I ever saw was Georgie, weighing over 4½ lb (2.2 kg): a giant among hogs. I heard of another called Fred who was just about to eat his 800th boiled egg, bringing him to about 3 lb 3 oz (1,800 g). Hedgehogs on the Continent are much bigger than ours, and even wild hedgehogs seem to attain similarly massive proportions without help.

The spines and skin

The spines are a hedgehog's most distinctive characteristic. They are just modified hairs, about 1" (2–3 cm) long and $^1/_{10}$" (2 mm) in diameter. They taper to a very sharp point at one end. At the other end, the spine narrows, bends through about 60° at the narrowest point – the 'neck' of the spine – and then ends in a

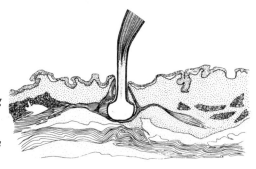

Vertical section through the skin of a hedgehog showing 'neck' and bulbous base of a spine and the many small skin muscles

hemispherical bulb which is buried in the skin. This arrangement means that if the hedgehog is struck a blow or falls heavily on to its spines, the force is absorbed by bending the springy spine 'necks'. Moreover, the ball buried in the skin forms a big blunt end which prevents the spine being forced back into the animal's own flesh: very useful adaptations.

Inside, the spines are hollow with strengthening ridges running down the inside walls of the tube. This provides a very strong and rigid structure with little weight.

Whole spine

Cross section of spine

Each spine is a creamy white, shading to brown at the base and pure white at the tip. Just behind the sharp end is a dark band, usually chocolate brown, which gives the spiny coat an overall grizzled appearance. In young hedgehogs (and occasional old ones too) the dark band is almost black, giving a very contrasty look to the spines.

It is quite common for a few individual spines to be all-white (often in younger animals), and some hedgehogs have patches of white spines, a characteristic which can probably be inherited. Occasionally we see hedgehogs *all* of whose spines are white or yellowish, making the animal look like a ghost. These are just colour variants; in other respects they are quite normal, with brown hairs, dark feet and black eyes. True albinos are sometimes seen too. These have no dark colouration anywhere, not even a black nose; their eyes are characteristically pale pink.

Probably fewer than one in 10,000 hedgehogs deviate so markedly from the normal coloration, and white hedgehogs are probably rarer than white moles. Whereas some mammals (e.g. squirrels and mice) occasionally produce all-black colour varieties, hedgehogs never do. I have seen blue ones and an orange one, but these were a consequence of tangling with newly painted garden fences.

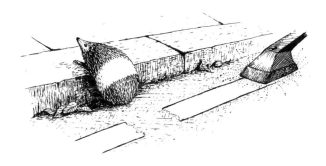

In 1898 a Professor Fritsch reported to a scientific society that he had obtained a spineless variety of the hedgehog. He exhibited a stuffed specimen and published a photograph of it. But I suspect that someone had been pulling Herr Professor's leg. His specimen was a hedgehog all right, you can see the distinctive teeth in his photograph, but the lack of spines was more likely to have been due to a mischievous taxidermist than a natural phenomenon. It would be comparatively simple to cut away the spiny skin of a dead hedgehog, sew up the remaining edges along the animal's back and create a stuffed improbability just like the professor's photograph.

The hedgehog is not spiny on the underside of course (otherwise it couldn't roll up). The chest, throat, belly and legs are all covered by a long and rather coarse grey-brown fur. Where this meets the spiny area, along the flanks, the fur is extra long and shaggy. This creates the impression of a skirt, fringing the edge of the hedgehog's body. The belly fur is very sparse and you can easily see the skin through it – not like in rabbits or cats for example. This must make it a chilly business for the hedgehog to forage in frosty conditions or in dew-laden grass, especially as its spiny parts have no soft fur at all. Hedgehogs are unusual in having so little insulation for their bodies. On the other hand coarse, sparse hair does not get clogged by mud like an ordinary mammal's fur, not will it collect plant burrs or become heavily saturated with wet. Perhaps the advantages of a hairy belly, for one so close to the ground, outweigh the disadvantages of heat loss and discomfort.

How many spines does a hedgehog have?

By the time a baby hedgehog leaves its mother's nest, it has about 3,000 spines on its back. As it grows older and bigger, more spines are added to maintain a suitable density of them. Consequently an average adult hedgehog weighing about 1 lb 5 oz (600 g) has a total of 5,000 or so spines. A very big animal, over twice that size, may have 7,500 spines. It is unlikely that many more would be found. Some books suggest that hedgehogs have 16,000 spines but this is an exaggerated figure, probably based on a faulty method of estimation.

Do hedgehogs moult?

All mammals have hair and it is normal to moult periodically as a means of getting rid of old hairs and replacing them with new ones: for example, the hedgehog's relatives, the shrews and moles, moult twice per year. The long, thick winter coat is shed in spring to be replaced by summer fur. In the autumn, this is lost and a new winter coat is grown as longer denser fur becomes more necessary.

The hedgehog is less concerned to keep itself warm in winter and would find it highly inconvenient to moult all its spines twice a year; they would take too long to replace. In practice, hedgehogs moult the same way that we humans do. Each hair and spine follicle has its own rate of growth and is not synchronized with its neighbours. So spines and hairs are being grown and lost continuously: one or two at a time, not in a big co-ordinated seasonal moult. In shrews and moles an individual hair has a 'service life' of only six months till the next moult. In few mammals do the individual hairs persist longer than a year. But each of the hedgehog's spines may last well over a year, perhaps more than 18 months before it finally falls out and a replacement is grown.

The hedgehog's body: from the inside

Most of the anatomical interest of the hedgehog is on the outside, in its spines and skin. Inside, the body is equipped with a standard set of mammal bones and guts which are fairly unremarkable. In fact the skeleton is so ordinary and unspecialized that it resembles in many ways that of the simplest prototype mammals that existed over 50 million years ago.

The feet all have five toes and the forearm contains two separate bones – features which are lost or at least modified in more highly evolved mammals. The principal variation from the norm in the skeleton is the shortness of the neck, though it still contains the same number of vertebrae (7) as other mammals, including humans. Presumably this makes it easier for the hedgehog to roll up into a compact ball.

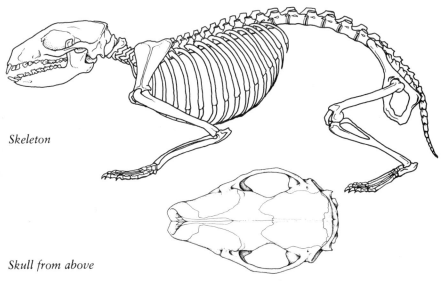

Skeleton

Skull from above

The skull is broad and strong, squared-off at the front and with well formed cheek bones (in contrast to the skulls of relatives like shrews and moles). The teeth are very odd. The two big incisors at the front of the lower jaw (used for picking up prey) lie almost flat and point forwards instead of upwards. They don't therefore form a sharp cutting edge: one reason why the hedgehog's bite is pretty harmless. In the upper jaw, there is a big gap between the front teeth:

another reason for not fearing a nasty bite from them. What appear to be large canine teeth sticking down from the upper jaw are actually special incisors; the real canines lie further back and are quite small. The rest of the teeth are sharply pointed, just the thing for chomping up tough beetles. There are 36 teeth altogether, but fewer in babies. Hedgehogs, like humans, have milk teeth when they are young; the last of these is usually lost at an age of three or four months and the adult dentition is complete well before the animal's first birthday. Eating gritty food such as worms blunts the teeth and in old animals they tend to be quite worn. However, it is very unusual to find a hedgehog with teeth that are worn-out or missing. Presumably, once they reach that stage, they cannot feed properly and will soon die.

The hedgehog's soft innards need not concern us. Suffice to say that there is over a metre of guts, plus a very large stomach: plenty of room to stow away a generous helping of bread and milk. The hedgehog seems to have strong digestive juices, which help to cope with a very varied diet, but this does mean that dead hedgehogs decay quickly and soon begin to pong.

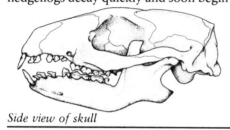

Side view of skull   Front view of skull

Do hedgehogs bite?

Yes, they do bite, but it's nothing to get in a stew about. In fact it is such a rare event as to be of considerable interest. Of all the many hundreds of hedgehogs I have handled only five have ever bitten me. Two of these were other people's 'tame' hedgehogs who happened to take a particular dislike to me, and one (Emily) always tried to bite me whenever I gave her the chance. She never bit anyone else, just me, and on one occasion did so as I recorded a TV programme about how nice hedgehogs are. The film shows me chatting away with Emily savaging my finger with considerable determination! This incident demonstrates not only composure on my part, but also that the hedgehog's bite is really not a serious matter.

Each time a hedgehog has bitten me, it has done so slowly and with great deliberation, allowing plenty of time for me to avoid trouble if I wished. Moreover, the long, weak jaws and peculiar gap in the hedgehog's front teeth (see p. 27) meant that blood was never drawn, even when I was bitten in some soft spot like the skin between my fingers. Only a few tooth marks remained, even after half a minute's assault. The prickles are more uncomfortable than the teeth. It's not like being bitten by a rat, weasel or squirrel, for example—they are the professionals. They bite fast, hard and deep and are really quite nasty. By comparison the hedgehog is a feeble amateur biter.

The rolling-up mechanism

Rolling up into a defensive ball is a very characteristic piece of hedgehog behaviour. No other mammal does it so completely or so effectively. The action is brought about by the contraction of special muscles in the skin. Firstly, a pair of muscles pull the skin forward over the head, and another pair pull it backwards over the animal's bottom. Then a big circular muscle operates like the drawstring of a duffel bag. It runs round the animal's body at the edge of the spiny part of the skin (which is very baggy and extra voluminous). As it contracts, it draws the spiny skin downwards and tightly closes it; forcing legs, head and tail inside. The result is a tightly contracted ball, completely enveloped in the spiny skin. The head is tucked up against the tail; there is no way in. A hedgehog can stay like this tirelessly for hours; contracting a bit tighter when danger is imminent.

Rolling-up muscles: thick muscles under the skin help a hedgehog roll up into a tight ball

As a further defence, tiny skin muscles are attached to the ball-like ends of all the individual spines. When they contract too, the spines are made to bristle and point rigidly in all directions like a mass of barbed wire. In this state hedgehogs are so well protected that they probably have fewer natural enemies than any other mammal of this size (see p. 85).

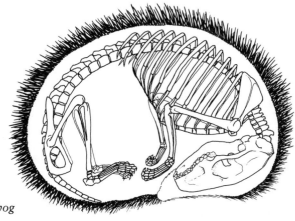

X-ray view of rolled-up hedgehog

However, it is comparatively unusual for a hedgehog to roll up completely into a ball. They do it if attacked, some do it if they are picked up, but their usual reaction to threat is merely to hunch themselves up, tuck the head in and move the skin forwards with spines bristling to protect the face. Only when the animal is picked up or bowled over will it go to the next stage of pulling in its feet and drawing the spiny skin tightly right around itself. Some hedgehogs are surprisingly tolerant (or lazy) and do not adopt this full defensive posture unless it is really necessary; they scurry away from danger and don't roll up at all.

Fleas

The hedgehog has a well deserved reputation for being flea-ridden. It is very unusual to find one with no fleas on it and sometimes there may be up to 500 on a single animal. What makes this appear even worse is the fact that the coarse hair and widely spaced spines do nothing to hide the fleas from our horrified gaze. The fleas seem all the more numerous because they are so conspicuous and constantly on the move. Even when there are only a few fleas present, as is normal, the hedgehog still appears to be over-endowed with 'little friends'.

Fleas can jump over 100 times their own height (equivalent to a man jumping over London's Post Office Tower!); but most of the time they scurry about in a frantic, hurried manner among the hedgehog's belly and facial hairs. To help in its rapid movement through this hairy jungle, the flea's body is very narrow and also very smooth and shiny.

Just because hedgehogs often have lots of fleas and these are very conspicuous, it doesn't mean that hedgehogs are the source of all fleas. Their reputation in that respect is wholly undeserved. People often say, 'Oh, my dog's got fleas again. He must have found a hedgehog.' This is a wickedly unjust accusation. If your dog has fleas, then it probably got them from another dog (or perhaps some other mammal). It isn't fair to blame the hedgehog. The only way to be even half certain of where the fleas have come from is to get them identified by an expert.

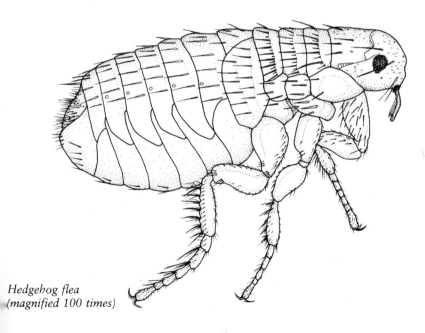

*Hedgehog flea
(magnified 100 times)*

The point is that in Britain we have over 50 different kinds of fleas, half of them only found on bats and birds. Many of the others are 'host specific', that is to say they live on only one type of animal and very rarely on any other species. The hedgehog flea (scientifically known as *Archaeopsylla erinacei*) is one of these. It lives on hedgehogs, sometimes on foxes and only very occasionally on other things. It is easy to understand why. The hedgehog's skin is a peculiar micro-habitat. The fleas are accustomed to the bare skin, draughty spaces between the spines, and harsh fur. If they find themselves in the dense, warm, fluffy coat of a cat or dog, they must immediately know that they are in the wrong habitat. It would be just like taking a grouse from the open moors and putting it in a dense thicket of trees – very upsetting! Consequently, hedgehog fleas do not remain on wrong hosts, but drop off and hope to find another hedgehog. The same goes for hedgehog fleas which get on to humans. They will do this (especially if made to jump or if they are leaving the body of a fresh-dead hedgehog) and they will bite; but they do not stay long before leaving to find a proper host.

The reverse is also true; the hedgehog's skin is such a peculiar environment that fleas from other species don't like to live there. Consequently you very rarely find any other types of flea on the hedgehog. I have collected over 2,000 fleas from many hedgehogs and only one of them was not the special hedgehog flea (it was a mole flea).

Fleas feed by sucking blood and sometimes, for reasons that are not fully understood, their digestive system goes haywire causing them to excrete blood as a brown, gooey mess on the hedgehog's spines. This leads to a curious condition seen in the summer when some hedgehogs seem to have lots of blood on their spines but no obvious wounds from which it could have come.

Getting rid of fleas

If you want to get rid of the fleas, when keeping a pet hedgehog for example, it is easily done using the commercially available flea powders sold by pet shops. The powder should be lightly dusted among the hedgehog's spines, taking care to avoid the animal's eyes. Naturally it is difficult to get the powder on to the hedgehog's belly when it is rolled up, but there is no need to try too hard. Powder will shake off in the nest and bedding, soon killing the remaining fleas as the hedgehog moves about.

In the wild, fleas breed in the nest, not on the body of their host. Baby flea larvae grow up in the nest lining, so if you are keeping a pet hedgehog for a while, it is a good idea to change the animal's bedding occasionally to get rid of these lodgers.

People often worry that depriving a hedgehog of its fleas might be harmful in some way, but why should it? Would you mind? In fact, as hedgehogs appear completely indifferent to the presence of their fleas (even lots of them), it is hardly likely that they will be unduly bothered by their absence.

Hedgehogs in New Zealand have no fleas.

A nasty problem

One of the nastiest and most upsetting experiences is to find a hedgehog with small maggots in its skin, especially around the eyes. This looks particularly horrible and, sadly, is not uncommonly seen in sickly baby hedgehogs especially in late summer.

What seems to happen is that the hedgehog becomes ill and lethargic, its body temperature falls and flies mistake it for dead and lay their eggs (these little white things are sometimes found in the fur and should be swabbed with dilute disinfectant and combed out). The eggs may hatch before the hedgehog is actually dead and lead to the distressing sight of a maggoty animal. It is probably kindest to kill the hedgehog, especially if its eyes are affected, even though it will not itself show any signs of concern for its plight. By careful cleaning with disinfectant the situation may be retrieved, but the hedgehog is likely to die anyway from other causes. It may not, but the omens aren't good.

Ticks and their removal

Ticks are distant relatives of spiders. The adult form has a shiny grey globular body, almost about half an inch (a centimetre) long. There are eight tiny legs at the front end and a set of mouthparts which dig into the hedgehog's skin to suck blood. These rather nasty animals can be made to let go and drop off by touching their back end with a burning cigarette. They can also be tweaked off with forceps, but this needs practice or you leave the mouthparts stuck in the hedgehog's skin. To avoid such a mishap leading to a septic wound, the skin should be swabbed with alcohol or disinfectant. Sometimes dousing with disinfectant alone will make the ticks let go.

Left alone, the ticks will feed on the hedgehog's blood for a while then drop off of their own accord, but it is best to kill them if you can to avoid their getting on to pets.

One hedgehog may have several ticks on its body, but most have none. Sometimes young larval ticks may be found; small, flat, orange-brown things. Unlike fleas, these do not jump or run about. They can be pulled off with tweezers; but as with fleas, the hedgehog makes no attempt to get rid of its passengers for itself.

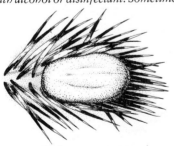

Tick among spines

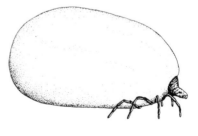

Adult tick

Hedgehog's voice

Normally hedgehogs are silent except for gentle twittering and snuffling as they poke about seeking food. Louder snorting accompanies their courtship rigmarole (p. 46). However, on rare occasions, the hedgehog can let loose the most awful noise. It sounds like a very loud pig squeal. I have heard it only twice; both times when the animal was apprehensive about being handled – though I wasn't actually hurting it. The scream was certainly most alarming and might occasionally serve to put off a would-be predator. Young hedgehogs sometimes make squeaky noises and I recently heard a juvenile (barely old enough to have left the nest) make a series of very loud, bird-like chirp-chirp-chirp noises. Again this seems to be comparatively unusual.

Recently it has been reported that male East African hedgehogs emit a little 'song' of twittering noises during courtship, but nobody has recorded this behaviour in British hedgehogs.

Hedgehog senses

We humans depend very much on our eyes for information about our surroundings. Most of our mental pictures are visual ones, so it is hard to imagine life as a hedgehog in which vision is comparatively unimportant and smell is the primary sense.

Hedgehogs certainly aren't blind; their little black eyes can spot your approach in the dark from a fair distance away. They also learn to recognize major landmarks like trees and houses. Probably these register as distinctive shapes silhouetted against the sky. With eyes so close to the ground, practically everything will be seen that way. The mechanism of the hedgehog's eye is such that it can see things in front of its nose, but probably not in much detail and certainly not in full colour. The hedgehog's view of the world is probably like that of an old box camera: limited in scope and portrayed in shades of brown and cream. In daylight the eyes work a little better and are capable of distinguishing some colours, but of course they are rarely given the chance because hedgehogs are nocturnal.

Under normal circumstances, the hedgehog relies heavily on its nose to find things and probably gets out of the habit of using its eyes much. Consequently its behaviour sometimes looks to us very short-sighted and stupid as it walks past juicy food or towards potential danger without apparently noticing what it is doing.

Smell is all important: by smell the hedgehog mainly finds its food, recognizes other hedgehogs and senses the presence of danger (it can detect a person many yards away if the wind is in the right direction). Everywhere it goes, the hedgehog is constantly sniffing the ground or pointing its nose skyward to test the air. Food can be detected, even under 1" (3 cm) of soil. The 'smell centres' in the hedgehog's brain are large, indicating their importance. It is quite likely that the hedgehog's nose plays a major role in its social life, helping to recognize other hedgehogs and to distinguish sex and social status, even at a distance, in a way that we do with our eyes.

Many other nocturnal animals have long sensitive whiskers, but although the hedgehog does have a few of these sensory hairs on its snout, they are neither big nor important in its life. Ears are another matter. Though small (only about

½"/1 cm long) and barely poking out of the fur, they are very sensitive. They play an important role in detecting prey; to a hedgehog even worms are probably quite noisy things as they move about. The hedgehog can detect a wide range of sounds and its ability to detect high pitched notes is probably similar to our own. It is particularly sensitive to abrupt sounds like clicks; a handclap will make it flinch instantly, and the sound of a camera shutter is usually sufficient to cause a sharp ducking of the head and bristling of the spines, blurring the photograph.

The curious case of No. 28

No. 28 was one of the hedgehogs we radio-tracked in our garden study (see p. 71). He was almost blind. He showed no reaction to torchlight, frequently ran over our feet and often bumped into things. When he visited a particular food bowl, he sometimes fell off the patio where it was placed. He usually entered and left the garden by the gate, but if this were closed he would crash full tilt into it before turning to one side and using a route under the fence. Of all the hedgehogs we studied, he would surely have been the most likely one to become dependent on food put out by
kindly people and surely he, more than any other hedgehog, might have been expected to live as near a food bowl as he could. In fact he travelled considerable distances (at least 1.2 miles/2 km. a night) often at very high speed. He often ran so fast his legs were an almost invisible blur and we could hardly keep up with him. He 'courted' female hedgehogs frequently and with vigour; he fought off another that sought to share his food bowl. In short, he managed to be a very competent hedgehog in spite of his disability.

Can hedgehogs taste?

They certainly can, yet to our way of thinking they don't seem very discriminating. For example they will eat badly decomposing carrion, but perhaps that's the equivalent of eating smelly cheese. They will also eat millipedes and certain beetles that exude a
nasty chemical to protect themselves from just such a fate. Some pet hedgehogs become very fastidious and develop exacting tastes causing considerable problems for their owners, refusing to eat anything other than tasty (and expensive) mealworms, for example.

Are hedgehogs intelligent?

Basically the answer to this question has to be 'no', though it does depend on what we mean by 'intelligent'. Certainly hedgehogs do not have powers of reasoning and cannot be expected to solve problems of the kind that chimpanzees sort out. If a hedgehog does overcome a particularly difficult set of circumstances, it probably is the result of chance or trial and error. The solution is unlikely to be remembered and used again.

On the other hand, pet hedgehogs can be taught very simple tasks such as choosing between a black and a white trap door, if food is always placed behind one but not the other. Similarly they will learn to distinguish between shapes and symbols; but only to a limited extent. Some hedgehogs will also learn to come when their names are gently called. Few attempts have been made to train hedgehogs more fully than this and there are no reports that suggest that their abilities are any greater than those of rats.

It is certainly true that hedgehogs are individually very variable in their behaviour and personality. This is probably an important aspect of their social behaviour in the wild. In captivity it is noticeable that some hedgehogs are tame from the start, whilst others never even uncurl without signs of acute nervousness. Some captive hedgehogs are similar to dogs and cats in that they will behave in a relaxed way with their normal keeper, but never settle down with anyone else. Even hedgehogs in the same litter grow up with different personalities.

There are plenty of stories which show that hedgehogs have reasonably good memories, especially for places. For example, one animal that was used to living indoors, always sleeping in one place and always being fed near the kitchen stove, was sent to live elsewhere for several months. On her return she immediately behaved as though she had never been away, and knew exactly where to find nest box and food.

It is interesting that memory survives hibernation. During winter the brain is almost completely shut down and inactive (unlike our own brain during normal sleep) yet whatever mechanism enables memories to be stored is not wrecked by the drastic changes in temperature and activity.

Simple tricks to try and teach to a hedgehog

1. Pulling food into the cage. Put a piece of favourite food on a flat plastic strip (e.g. a ruler or tape). Start with this adjacent to the bars, so that the animal learns to nibble food outside the cage. Then place it further away, forcing the hedgehog to learn to pull the strip towards the cage before it can have its reward. If it gets the hang of this problem, gradually lengthen the strip to see how far away the animal is able to recognize food and how hard it is willing to work in order to get it. Some birds will learn a similar trick very quickly and a hedgehog has learnt to pull in food from 12" (30 cm) away.

2. Keep a hedgehog in a large box or pen. Construct a barrier with two sliding or hanging doors in it. This should span the width of the pen and be too tall for the hedgehog to climb over (i.e. 1 foot/30 cm at least). Beyond the doors the pen should be divided down the middle with wire mesh to form two parallel corridors, food being available at the end of one. Colour the two doors differently and always put food behind the same colour door. When the hedgehog has got used to always going through (say) the left hand black door instead of the right hand white door, swap the doors over. Does it still go to the left door or to the black door? Repeat the experiment using doors of the same colour to see if your hedgehog can tell right from left. Use the coloured doors, swapping them randomly from left to right (but always have the food behind the same colour) to see if it's the colour the hedgehog recognizes, not the side.

NB *Make sure the food is at the far end of the corridor and not so near the door the animal can smell which door it is behind.*

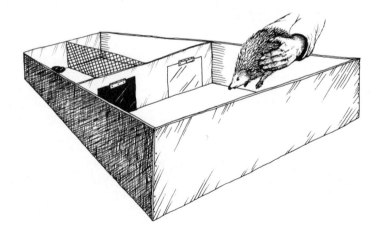

Strange behaviour: self-anointing and other funny goings-on

One of the most extraordinary activities that a hedgehog performs has been christened 'self-anointing'. Certain hedgehogs will suddenly abandon normal behaviour and begin to produce large quantities of frothy saliva. Then, with great smacking of the lips, they will proceed to use their tongues to flick this white foam over their backs and flanks. To reach the more difficult places, like the middle of the back, a hedgehog will twist and contort itself to a grotesque shape, protruding its tongue to a quite extraordinary degree. Sometimes this self-anointing will only last a minute or two, occasionally the hedgehog will become almost obsessively engrossed, ignore all else and carry on for ten minutes or more. Then it suddenly stops and resumes normal activity.

It is a quite extraordinary performance, which leaves the animal flecked with foam, just like streaks of soap suds. It is not at all clear what starts the whole business off. Often it begins when the animal smells or chews something aromatic like furniture varnish or a cigar butt. Briefly chewing shoe leather often gets pet hedgehogs going. In the wild, hedgehogs do not necessarily encounter these stimulants, but may be triggered off by other things. However, the presence of a special chemical substance is not essential, sometimes distilled water is enough. Yet many hedgehogs, perhaps the majority, never seem to self-anoint at all. It's all very puzzling.

Theories have been advanced to explain this energetic and messy behaviour, most of them not very plausible. The idea that it was a method of getting rid of fleas doesn't seem correct – or if it is, it doesn't work. It is certainly not performed more often by flea-ridden animals and in fact is most commonly observed among pet hedgehogs which are kept scrupulously clean by their owners.

Chewing leather often sets them off

Another recent suggestion was that self-anointing was set off as a result of chewing toad skin (true) and that this contains poisonous substances (also true). The result would then be to distribute the toad skin poison in the hedgehog's frothy saliva all over the latter's spines. This would arm each spine with a poison tip, greatly increasing its defensive value. While this theory may be true (and its author provided experimental evidence by jabbing his own skin with clean and with 'poisoned' spines to study the comparative effect), it cannot be the full explanation for self-anointing. For a start, hedgehogs do not need toad skin, but will self-anoint after contact even with innocuous substances. Moreover, the hedgehog's spines are a very effective protection anyway.

I think self-anointing may be connected with scent. Suppose that the saliva contained a pheromone, a smelly substance recognized by other hedgehogs. (This is quite possible: male pigs have scent in their saliva.) Spreading the froth over the body would allow the spines and fur to act like an 'air wick' and disseminate scent on the air (moths have special feathery structures that perform this function). Thus a hedgehog could advertise its presence to others of its own species and perhaps thereby defend its territory or attract a mate. The spiny skin would be adequate defence against any predators that might also be attracted. Such an idea fits in well with what we know about hedgehog social behaviour, though it is difficult to explain why self-anointing occurs not only in both sexes but also in young hedgehogs too.

This is obviously an area deserving a lot more research. All we can say for certain is that self-anointing is probably unique to the hedgehog and that it is such an elaborate and energetic performance that it must serve some purpose; we just don't know what.

Running in circles

Another strange piece of reported hedgehog behaviour is the habit of running in circles. This should not be confused with the usual snorting, circling waltz performed by pairs of hedgehogs before mating. Running in circles is just that— running, not shuffling— following a circular track 10 or 15 yards in diameter. It is performed by a single hedgehog, all on its own, scooting round and round without evident boredom or self-consciousness for lap after lap. This may go on for an hour or more, sometimes on successive nights.

Some say it's a sign of frustration. If so then you'd expect captive hedgehogs to do it a lot of the time. The jokers say that hedgehogs run in circles because their left legs are shorter than the other two.

Such frenetic behaviour is surely not normal nor likely to be connected with any aspect of the hedgehog's customarily stoical habits. Could this be some kind of abnormal behaviour brought about by illness? An infection, for example, could upset the sense of balance and cause non-linearity of locomotory behaviour, like being drunk. But drunks don't run, nor do they go in endless repeated circles. Still, illness could be the clue.

It may be significant that running in circles seems to have been first reported in the 1960s and frequently observed since then. It is not mentioned in earlier books on hedgehogs, despite extensive reviews of other habits. Did the earlier writers simply fail to observe this distinctive, conspicuous and enigmatic activity or is it something that hedgehogs have only started to do recently? The 1960s and 1970s were a period when large quantities of increasingly diverse chemicals were manufactured for use against garden pests. These substances are supposedly 'safe', but they are only tested on a limited range of animals (which doesn't include hedgehogs). It is known that certain chemicals may affect one species but not another. Could running in circles be a symptom of some kind of poisoning? Let's hope not and that it's just another bit of mysterious hedgehog behaviour in need of investigation.

The hedgehog's menu: the natural diet

Nowadays many hedgehogs must get a lot of their food off a plate in people's gardens (feeding garden hedgehogs is discussed further on p. 70 and feeding them in captivity is described on p. 56). However, their normal method of feeding is to quarter the ground meticulously, poking their noses into tussocks and crannies, seeking anything edible. Damp, grazed grassland is probably one of the best hunting grounds and hedgehogs may travel some distance to a good feeding place.

In the dark it is difficult to see what a hedgehog eats, though eager crunching noises suggest when a beetle is being devoured, while slobbery lip-smacking is more indicative of earthworms and slugs. Close inspection of the finger-sized black droppings, so often left on our lawns, shows glistening bits of beetles to be particularly frequent prey items.

Hedgehog dropping

A study by Dr Derek Yalden of Manchester University (still the only detailed investigation of British hedgehog diets) listed all the identifiable items found in 137 hedgehog stomachs collected from animals killed by gamekeepers or run over on the road. Beetles, such as cockchafers, weevils and dung beetles, were found in three quarters of the stomachs; testimony to the importance of these as hedgehog food. Over half the stomachs contained earwigs; caterpillars and slugs were also very frequent prey. Sometimes quite large numbers had been eaten by one animal in a very short time: 63 caterpillars in one case, 22 earwigs in another and 75 beetles in another. These creatures would be at the very top of every gardener's 'hit list', so it's obvious that hedgehogs must do a lot of good in gardens and farmland. It is likely that each hedgehog kills at least a hundred such invertebrates, many of them pests, in a night's foraging and thousands every year.

Earthworms are often taken of course; but, more surprisingly, so are large numbers of millipedes. These creatures produce nasty-tasting chemicals which are meant to deter predators from eating them. Certainly shrews eat few millipedes, but hedgehogs gobble them with relish, along with supposedly 'distasteful' ground beetles. It's not that hedgehogs have no sense of taste; simply that they are not put off by the chemical defences of these invertebrates. It may even be that these very same chemicals taste and smell so strongly as to actually help the hedgehog find the creatures that produce them: a counter-productive defence.

In short, it seems that hedgehogs will eat anything edible that they can find, but there are some notable exceptions to this. They seem to eat very few snails,

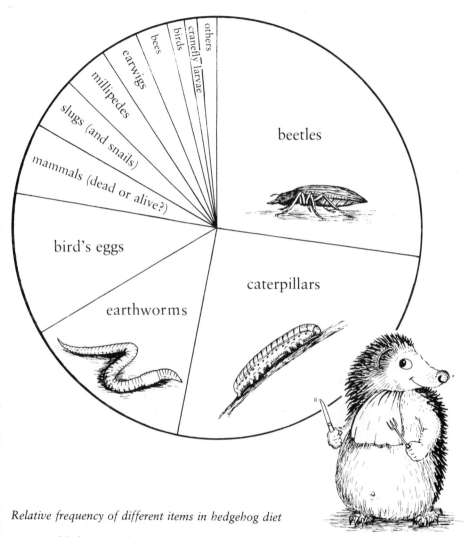

others
cranefly larvae
birds
bees
earwigs
millipedes
slugs (and snails)
mammals (dead or alive?)
bird's eggs
earthworms
beetles
caterpillars

Relative frequency of different items in hedgehog diet

presumably because their jaws are not able to cope with the shell. Hedgehogs also rarely eat centipedes, probably because these can bite and they can run fast too. Grasshoppers, despite their abundance, contribute little to the hedgehog's fare; again probably because they can leap away too fast to catch.

Mice and voles are probably eaten quite often, especially nestlings. Adults too may be consumed either as carrion or caught alive when cornered in a confined space (e.g. under a shed). Shrews and moles are eaten, even though these have distasteful skin glands (which is why cats will play with these animals but rarely eat them). Nine of Derek Yalden's hedgehogs had eaten bits of rabbit, probably found lying about as carrion. However, there have been astonishing tales told of hedgehogs actually chasing baby rabbits, rats and chickens and even killing them. This is hard to believe, partly because hedgehogs don't run fast enough and partly because their jaws and teeth are not suited to big-time carnivory. Nevertheless baby rabbits are pretty silly and if a hedgehog did once manage to grab hold of an unwary one, it could hang on or perhaps roll up around its victim and spike it on its spines.

The biggest mystery must surely be that hedgehogs seem to eat very few woodlice. This is odd because woodlice are very common creatures, especially in gardens. They can't be too distasteful to eat because shrews often take them. Nor is it that they are too small because hedgehogs often eat tiny bugs and daddy longlegs that have far less meat on them than woodlice. It may be that woodlice are too difficult to pick up in the hedgehog's teeth. A few simple observations ought to clarify that point.

Bits of grass and the odd leaf are often swallowed along with worms and other prey. Hedgehogs will also eat squashy fruit and of course bread and milk (see p. 74); but their main diet consists of animal material. Mostly this comprises the invertebrates mentioned above, but also vertebrates such as lizards and the occasional frog.

Certainly a more predaceous side to the hedgehog's character is revealed when the chicks of ground-nesting birds are encountered. Gulls, terns, gamebirds and doubtless pipits and skylarks all must lose a few broods to hedgehogs. Eggs are eaten too, usually leaving a mess of broken shells, stomped into a mixture of yolk and nest lining. It is precisely because of such depredations that gamekeepers regard the hedgehog as an enemy, but whenever careful studies have been made it has become clear that hedgehogs are insignificant predators. They may account for two or three per cent of clutches lost, one tenth of the numbers taken by foxes and really not enough to warrant all the fuss made by gamekeepers (see p. 99).

Hedgehogs, tins and drink containers

Not long ago it was reported in the press that some hedgehogs had discovered that civil servants discarded large numbers of disposable plastic tea and coffee cups round the grounds of a government research station. The cups contained lovely sweet and creamy dregs, well worth poking your head in as far as possible to lick up. But once inside, a hedgehog's spines are pressed tight against the walls of the cup, tighter still as it tries to push further in to lick up the last little bits. Then of course, as the head is withdrawn, the spines jam into the cup and the hedgehog is stuck with a plastic cup on its head. Numbers of bemused, helmeted hedgehogs were reported wandering about. A similar unfortunate was reported from Orkney with its head wedged in a plastic yoghurt pot.

Given time, a hedgehog could probably use its front paws to split and rip off most disposable plastic cups, but not tins. Countless tins are opened by picnickers every year and thoughtlessly tossed away. These not only have juicy dregs much to a hedgehog's liking, but they also have a rough spiky rim which would grip the spines tightly like a collar and stop a hedgehog getting its head out from cans of a certain size. In Bexhill Museum there is a large stuffed hedgehog alongside the open, discarded tin of cream that had been its downfall. The moral of these stories is of course that hedgehogs shouldn't be so greedy and we ought to be less untidy with our litter.

Breeding and raising a family

The hedgehog's breeding season lasts from about April till September. The main period of activity is usually in May and June when the nights are warm. It is at this time that you are most likely to hear the loud, rhythmic snorting of 'courting' hedgehogs in the garden. So loud is the noise that people have often woken up and gone to their open bedroom windows to see what was going on out in the flower beds.

Male continually circles the female, often nudging her closely

'Courtship' is a grandiose term for what is actually a rather ill-tempered and seemingly tedious affair. What happens is that a male, encountering a female, will begin to circle round her. She, with dogged perversity, will turn to keep her flank towards him. Undeterred, he continues to press his suit, while she constantly rebuffs him. The pair of them repeatedly shuffle round and round in circles. This palaver may go on for hours, though usually ends abruptly and prematurely with one or other animal running off. The whole rigmarole is accompanied by the characteristic, regular puffing and snorting noises emitted mainly by the female as she repulses the male, though he may snort too.

Not surprisingly, all this noise tends to attract attention, and not just from householders woken from their sleep. Frequently other male hedgehogs turn up, perhaps intent on getting a slice of the action. Courtship is thus often interrupted by the arrival of a fresh suitor, whereupon there is a brief intermission while he is dealt with. The two males square up to each other and may indulge in head-butting, banging each other about; one may even be chased off. Sometimes the new male wins the sparring match, sometimes both lose because the female does a bunk while the two males are squaring up to each other.

There is an old joke which poses the question, 'How do hedgehogs mate?' The answer is, 'Carefully;' and this is not far from the truth. With such a spiny partner, mating is not something to be undertaken lightly or without considerable

Courtship is often interrupted while an intruder is chased off

co-operation from the female. In fact she has to adopt a special posture, belly pressed flat to the ground, and back arched downwards so that her nose points skywards. Her spines must be laid flat. Neglect of any of these factors renders mating impossible and at any time the female can bristle her spines or throw the male off. For his part the male mounts the female from behind, gripping the spines over her shoulders with his teeth and scrabbling with his paws to get a better position. His own back must be arched into a most unhedgehog-like shape in order to get all the angles right for successful mating. And after all that, conception falls well short of a sure-fire certainty. Many females still fail to become pregnant, even after several matings, and a fair proportion may escape becoming pregnant altogether.

There is no evidence that any sort of pair bond is formed between male and female hedgehogs (though this has been suggested by some writers). The male stays with the female after mating for only a few hours, if that. Sometimes he (or she) may pair up with another partner the very same night. Complete promiscuity appears to be the rule. A study by Nigel Reeve showed that one male courted at least ten different females (some several times each) in two seasons and one female might have a dozen different mates.

Hedgehogs are not sexually mature in the year of their birth, so do not indulge in this sort of thing until their second year. They are then capable of breeding every year until their death.

Telling t'other from which

It is often assumed that the big, 'purposeful' hedgehogs are males; they might be, but you can't be certain, any more than you can tell the sexes from the shape of the head. People who assert that it's a 'he' or a 'she' are fooling themselves unless they check.

Sexing hedgehogs is easy; it's getting them to uncurl that's the problem.

Gently lift a hunched hedgehog, sliding your two hands under it, one from each side. Then shuffle and toss it slightly into the air so that it uncurls a little to put its feet on to your hands to steady itself. Continue the gentle agitation, drawing your hands apart so that its front feet are on one hand and back feet on the other. After a while the hedgehog should be fully extended. Its front end can then be lifted, perhaps pressing its back against your own tummy at the same time. You can then carefully peep at its underside to compare with the diagrams here. At all times, move slowly and gently, keep your hands and fingers flat. If you are clumsy, the hedgehog will roll up, trapping your fingers inside, and that's painful! When you get the hang of it, 'hedgehog charming' is easy, though the occasional individual (and sometimes pregnant ones) may obstinately refuse to uncurl.

In adult male hedgehogs the penis appears as a large opening about where you would expect the navel to be; about

2" (5 cm) in front of the anus. In females the two openings are close together (only about ½"/1 cm apart) and near to the base of the tail. Baby hedgehogs are more difficult to sex, especially when they are only a couple of months old—but at this age it hardly matters.

Normally there are equal numbers of males and females in a population. However, if you take a sample of hedgehogs (e.g. by catching them in the garden or by collecting road casualties), the sex ratio is likely to be heavily biased towards males in the spring and early summer. This is not because there are more males, but simply due to the fact that they are more active at that time and therefore more likely to be found. Conversely, in the autumn females may predominate, apparently because males begin hibernating earlier, leaving more females to be caught. Baby hedgehogs occur in approximately equal numbers of both sexes at any time.

Female   Male

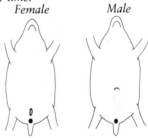

Family life

When a female does become pregnant, she will have her babies after about $4\frac{1}{2}$ weeks. Normally the gestation period of mammals is fairly fixed (9 months in humans for example), but in hedgehogs it is apparently rather variable. This may be due to the unpredictable British weather. A cold spell in the early spring may cause a shortage of food and a temporary resumption of hibernation. If the female went torpid, then the development of her embryos would be slowed down. When normal activity is resumed, embryo growth would pick up again but pregnancy would be lengthened by an amount corresponding to the period of torpor. This is only speculation; no research has been done on this intriguing possibility, but we do know that it happens in bats, who can be forced into 'summer hibernation' by cold weather and shortage of insect food, which imposes hibernation on bat embryos and lengthens the total time they take to develop. If something similar happened in hedgehogs it would be very unusual among mammals (and extremely interesting), but it would explain why hedgehog pregnancies seem to be of variable duration.

Most baby hedgehogs are probably born in June and July, perhaps a bit later in the north. Females that lose a litter for some reason, and also those that manage to raise a family early in the summer, are capable of conceiving a second litter. However, these are unlikely to be born before September and may come as late as October. They stand little chance of surviving.

The average family size is about 4 or 5, though some females have 6 or even 7 babies. So, theoretically, one mother hedgehog could have 10 or more young in a year; but this would be unusual. It is also unlikely that all of those young would survive. A more realistic expectation would be that the average mother manages to rear 2, perhaps 3 babies per season.

Giving birth to spiny babies could be a tricky business. Some books suggest that the problem is overcome by having very soft spines at birth; but even these would be a severe embarrassment if a baby was born tail first. It would just get stuck. This sometimes happens anyway, with fatal results. Normally the spines are covered by skin and appear just as little pimples on the surface. Soon after birth,

*Spines when
newly born are
hidden by pimples*

First set of spines is white with a parting down the middle

which only takes a minute or two, the baby's spines begin to appear. The first ones, about 100 of them, are pure white. They grow in two distinct tracts with a parting down the middle of the back from head to tail. Many books say the spines turn brown as the babies get older. This is wrong. The white spines stay white until they are moulted weeks or months later. What actually happens is that brown spines grow up among the white ones, wave after wave of them, until they swamp the first set. From about 15 days old, the white ones are hardly visible.

Dark spines grow up through the white

The babies are born into a specially constructed nest, often under a shed or pile of garden debris. The nest is like a large version of the winter nest, often made of leaves and grass and frequently incorporating bits of paper and other rubbish. No special material is collected to line it, though trampling around inside tends to soften and crumble the inner layers of the nest and ensure that the nest chamber is smooth inside. If the mother is disturbed within the first few hours of birth she is likely to desert or eat her babies. Later, when they are bigger, she may react to disturbance by carrying them off to another nest.

Baby hedgehogs are born blind and are pale pink. At 2 weeks old, their eyes open and by that time they not only have plenty of brown spines but their skin is also darker in colour. They have milk teeth, just like human babies, and these begin to be replaced in the third week of life. The last milk tooth is lost after about 4 months.

After a few days both white and brown spines are present

The mother feeds her babies on milk of course, for which purpose she has five pairs of nipples; easily enough outlets for the largest family. Nevertheless it's quite likely that available milk is sufficient to support no more than 4 or 5 young. In very dry or cold weather, the mother herself may be short of food and even less able to support her entire family. Probably about 1 in 5 of all baby hedgehogs die before they even leave the nest, members of larger litters being particularly at risk.

When they are 3 to 4 weeks old, young hedgehogs are big enough to leave the nest and go on foraging trips with the mother. A female leading a little procession of prickly babies is a charming sight and a welcome sign that they have survived one of the most difficult periods of their life. The babies soon learn what to eat, but return to the nest to take their mother's milk as well. Gradually, over a period

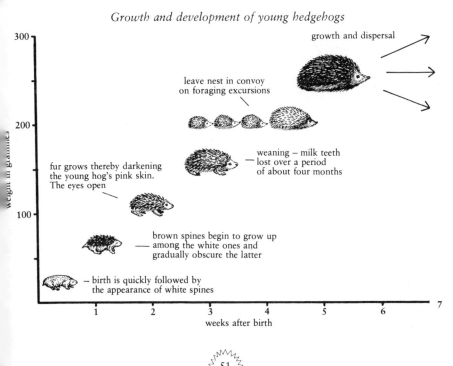

Growth and development of young hedgehogs

growth and dispersal

leave nest in convoy
on foraging excursions

weaning – milk teeth
lost over a period
of about four months

fur grows thereby darkening
the young hog's pink skin.
The eyes open

brown spines begin to grow up
among the white ones and
gradually obscure the latter

– birth is quickly followed by
the appearance of white spines

weight in grammes

weeks after birth

of about 10 days, the family splits up as the young ones wander off on their own. At this stage they weigh about 8 oz (250 g), ten times their weight at birth. From conception to weaning is only about 2 months. In that time each baby has been nourished mainly by milk from its mother. She has to provide enough nourishment for the 'manufacture' and maintenance of over 2 lb (a kilo) of hedgehogs (more than her own weight) as well as herself. It must be a tremendous strain and it is hardly surprising that twenty per cent of the young don't make it.

Once the family has dispersed, brothers and sisters are unlikely to meet again, for hedgehogs live solitary lives. Nor are they likely to meet their father because he has played no part in raising his offspring and it's difficult to see how he could ever recognize them as his own – and vice versa. Hedgehogs meet and pass each other like ships in the night. There's no more to it than that.

Autumn orphans

Some female hedgehogs give birth to late litters, in September or even October. By the time these babies are old enough to leave the nest, winter is nearly upon them. They are faced with the almost insuperable problem of finding enough to eat at the very time of year when nights are getting colder and natural food is becoming increasingly scarce. Wet and frosty nights just add to the misery.

The trouble is that the baby hedgehogs not only want enough food to live from day to day, but need extra in order to double their size in the space of a few weeks. On top of *that* they need still more food to store as fat to keep them going during hibernation: all at a time when food supplies are diminishing. Clearly they can't make ends meet. Under these circumstances it is common to see baby hedgehogs weighing only 5–7 oz (150–200 g) struggling against the odds to survive – often foraging in broad daylight. While the adults have long since gone into hibernation, these babies are forced to remain active well into the winter, even as late as Christmas. This is why the majority of hedgehogs seen after mid November seem to be small ones. The question is, what to do about them? The same goes for the nests of abandoned baby hedgehogs we sometimes find in the autumn during garden-tidying operations.

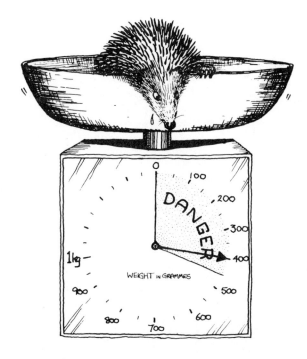

Can we help the young to survive? *Should* we help? Perhaps it would be cruel to interfere and prevent them from hibernating?

The answer to these questions is simple: if we leave the babies alone they will almost certainly die. Hedgehogs need a certain minimum amount of stored fat to see them safely through the winter; they should weigh about 1 lb (450 g). If they hibernate before reaching that weight they stand practically no chance of surviving. It follows then that to leave underweight baby hedgehogs to their own devices any time after late September effectively condemns them to death. Taking them into captivity and giving them artificial food may be unnatural, but at least they may live; they may even become quite tame (see next section for details of rearing baby hedgehogs).

Once the babies have attained the necessary weight they can be released. Preferably this should be done during a mild period so the shock is not too great. The important thing is to ensure that they have access to dry nesting material and a suitable place to build a winter home. Ideally this should be a woodland/shrubby area with plenty of leaves (see p. 94) but in your own garden, a sheet of hardboard propped against the fence or behind the shed would make a suitable shelter. Old newspaper forms an excellent substitute for leaves as nest material. Probably the hedgehog won't stay where you put it because it finds a better place – and that's all to the good.

Potential winter nest sites can be made against a wall or fence

Keeping hedgehogs and rearing babies

On the whole, hedgehogs don't make particularly good pets (being rather unresponsive creatures), but may be fun to keep for a while. Baby hedgehogs are often taken in by well meaning people and they may well owe their lives to their kindly foster parents. This particularly applies to underweight juveniles rescued from the oncoming winter. So some hints on hedgehog-keeping will not come amiss.

Hedgehogs will live in quite a small cage, less than half a square yard (metre) in area, but obviously prefer more space if possible. They can always be allowed out for exercise around the house, though they are often not well house trained. It is important that their cage or pen does not have bars or wire mesh on the floor; a hedgehog's feet are soft and will suffer damage unless a softer floor is provided. Newspaper, sawdust, earth, peat, even old carpet: all are suitable but need to be changed fairly frequently. Remember that hedgehogs can dig, so a simple pen in the garden won't hold them if they can tunnel under the walls. Remember too that they can climb. Wire mesh is easy, even boards or bricks are not escape-proof, though a strip of metal or plastic rainwater gutter fixed along the top of the walls offers a bulging smooth curve to climb over and can't easily be negotiated (but watch out at the corners). Although they are nocturnal in the wild, hedgehogs can be persuaded in captivity to emerge in daylight – by feeding during daytime.

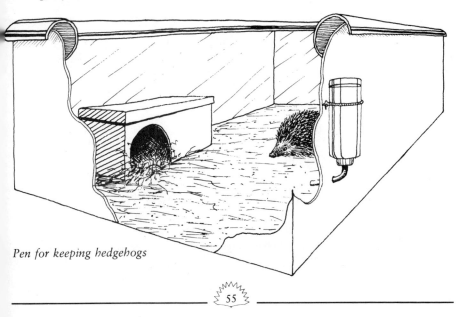

Pen for keeping hedgehogs

In the wild, hedgehogs drink often, so water should be available. If you give them an open bowl, they will stomp in it and make a mess. Use a water bottle from a pet shop, one that delivers water as drips. A wooden or cardboard box should be provided, lying on its side, and plenty of newspaper which the hedgehog will shred and carry to its box to make a nest. The nest box should have a roof or the nesting material becomes scattered.

Regular handling will persuade some animals to become very tame (see p. 48) for sexing and handling hedgehogs); but others remain totally intractable. It does no harm to remove ticks and fleas (see pp. 32, 33). Adult hedgehogs are no problem to look after and feed; the real difficulties come with trying to raise babies.

Sometimes a nest is accidentally disturbed in the garden revealing a mother and her family. They are best left alone and she will carry them to a fresh home. If no mother is present, or if babies are brought in by the dog, you may decide to try and rear them. If they are so young that they are still blind, there is little hope for them though they may survive if you are lucky. If they are old enough to have brown spines, there is a better chance of success. But don't be surprised if they die, hedgehogs are very vulnerable creatures until they are at least 6–8 weeks old.

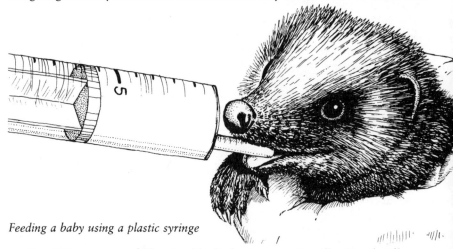

Feeding a baby using a plastic syringe

People have successfully raised hedgehogs on cow's milk, tinned milk, Complan and various baby foods, but the mother's milk is more than just food. For the first few days after birth, baby hedgehogs receive a lot of immune proteins in their milk supply and these help protect from infections and gut disorders. Cow's milk and other substitutes lack these ready-made natural medicines and so the young hedgehog is very susceptible to infections which may easily prove fatal. Liquid food should be offered from a pipette, a dropper or a plastic syringe. The hedgehogs will soon learn to drink from it, but will need feeding every few hours or so. They should be persuaded to lap from a dish as soon as possible, then they will be less trouble to look after.

When they are about 3 weeks old, with eyes open and a body weight of 4 oz (100 g) or more, baby hedgehogs should be persuaded to diversify their diet. Scrambled egg is a welcome treat; also bread soaked in gravy, the juice out of fresh liver; anything semi-liquid and rich in protein and as varied as possible. My hedgehogs rather liked crumbled chocolate biscuits in milk. Later they can graduate on to tinned dog food: two or three big tablespoonsful twice a day should be enough. This could become expensive and anyway the natural diet is very varied, so it is a good idea to 'dilute' or extend the dog food by mashing in puppy meal, table scraps or broken biscuits. Add a little water to stop the mixture being too dry. Healthy hedgehogs will thrive on a mixed diet like this and put on weight rapidly. One of mine, rescued as a baby from near death, was soon putting on weight at an average of $^1/_3$ oz (10 g) per day and ultimately grew to be the biggest one-year-old hedgehog I've ever seen; then he escaped!

Little hedgehog treats are always welcome, and here individual preferences become evident. Some love meal-worms (unfortunately, because they are expensive), others like bits of chicken. I heard of one that was partial to mandarin oranges and knew another that would do anything for salted peanuts. Perhaps oddest of all was Emily. She loved milk, so much so that when the BBC tried to film her eating worms, she would only oblige if they were first dipped in milk. She then attacked them eagerly, but only to lick the milk off; she left the worms.

You can perform some interesting experiments to determine hedgehog likes and dislikes. Unfortunately some individuals become very fussy and refuse to eat dog food and other sensible food and insist on a special diet. They should be discouraged from becoming too fixed on one particular thing, partly because it's a nuisance and partly because they are then likely to be less adaptable and able to look after themselves if they escape or are released.

However, food is only part of the problem with baby hedgehogs. For them, the secret of success is to keep them *warm*. This is vital. Babies have a large surface area through which they lose body heat, and next to no insulation to prevent this happening. If they cool down, then their bodily functions begin to get slower so digestion for example takes longer to release food energy. Their movements get slower, which means that the muscles produce less heat and the body cools still more. Quite soon the baby hedgehog is trapped in a downward spiral of getting colder and slower and it dies over a period of 2 or 3 days like a run-down clockwork toy. Obviously this is a major threat to babies on cold nights in late summer and early autumn, a time when shortage of food may leave them in trouble anyway. Even quite big hedgehogs may suffer this cooling down syndrome if they are sickly.

Warmth will stimulate them, raise their level of activity and may help them 'turn the corner' on to the road to viability. But do not provide warmth in the form of a desk lamp or something similar shining down. The best way is to wrap a hot water bottle in a couple of layers of blanket and let the hedgehogs nestle down on top or against it. This bathes them in all-round warmth without glaring light. Try to keep the temperature similar to that inside your own pockets by renewing the hot water every few hours. Give them clean blankets every couple of days.

Within a few weeks, young hedgehogs may grow fat enough to survive hibernation out of doors, but it will do them no harm if they are kept indoors without hibernating. It may be 'unnatural' not to hibernate but not cruel. Indeed since a good third of all hedgehogs probably die in hibernation, captive ones may well be better off without it.

If you decide to release your hedgehog, it is best to choose a place where they are likely to be reasonably common already: parks, old cemeteries, farmland, big gardens – places with plenty of worms, bushes and trees. Try to put out some food for a few nights after release to help introduction to new surroundings. Choose a period of warm, muggy weather if possible. This will help ensure that there is plenty of natural food about and your animal is not inconvenienced by being cold itself. Remember that hedgehogs need dry leaves and a sheltered place (e.g. bottom of hedge, under a shed, deep in a thicket) to build a good winter nest, so try to choose a place with these features too. Avoid the vicinity of busy roads if you can, but remember that hedgehogs wander far and wide so there's not much point in choosing one place rather than another just because it's 100 yards further away from traffic. They are not bothered about noise; two garden hedgehogs I studied chose daytime nests only 3 yards (metres) from a very busy dual carriageway with fast cars going by at a rate of 1 every 3 seconds.

Getting hedgehogs tame

Some hedgehogs are unco-operative and that's that. However, others will become very tame indeed, especially those that have been reared by hand from an early age. They will then not roll up or 'bristle' and will allow at least their owners to tickle their tummies and turn them upside down, feet in the air; things that normally meet with severe hedgehog disapproval. I know one animal (Georgie, star of the BBC-TV film) who would come out of her nest box when called by name; but another (Emily, who had also been hand reared) who often bit me.

There is so much individuality among hedgehogs that one cannot generalize and say 'this is right' or 'this is wrong'. However, as a rule, sudden noises and clumsy handling are the two things most likely to upset hedgehogs. They normally don't like bright lights either. Regular handling is helpful: firm, but gentle. Avoid touching their faces and sudden movements, especially towards the belly. Handling when they are fed is a good idea; they then associate you with food. The next step is to reward good behaviour with some favourite morsel – the problem being that hedgehogs' tastes differ. Georgie loved salted peanuts, Emily liked milk, others are eager for mealworms while some won't bother with them.

Hedgehogs out and about

When moving about, hedgehogs look uncannily like clockwork toys. This is becauses the body is surrounded by a fringing 'skirt' of long hair which hides the feet. The animal also walks with its legs bent in such a way that the whole body is low-slung and close to the ground, again concealing the feet. Hedgehogs thus move as though on hidden wheels, without visible signs of propulsion. It then comes as a surprise to discover that hedgehogs can run quite fast. They raise themselves up on straighter legs and make a bee-line for some distant objective, reaching average speeds of 30–40 metres per minute: nearly 2 miles per hour. To us, this is only a fast walking pace, but in the hedgehog it looks and *is* really rapid. Thirty metres is 150 times the animal's own length. Moreover, some hedgehogs keep up an average speed of this sort for several minutes at a stretch, including short sprints of 2 metres per second (6 m.p.h.) or more; about the maximum speed we can walk without breaking into a run. Careful study has shown that the average speed of male hedgehogs in the course of a night's wanderings is nearly twice the average speed of females.

Despite these occasional bursts of athleticism, the hedgehog's normal gait is a patient, unflappable trundle. Again, this gives the misleading impression that the hedgehog is unlikely to dig, climb or do anything else dramatic. They certainly can dig, but don't usually bother except to escape by excavating a scrape under a fence or some other obstacle.

They can climb too, though it's not clear why they bother. Hedgehogs have been found in upstairs bedrooms, having arrived via the staircase or even, Errol Flynn-style, up the ivy clad wall and in through the open window. At least one hedgehog has been found hibernating in a thatched roof and there are stories of hedgehogs reaching roof gutters by squeezing up the inside of drainpipes. They

Errol Hog

will, in mountaineering spirit, 'chimney' up a house, bracing themselves in the gap between a downpipe and the angle of a wall. Mere wire fences are a doddle and even wooden slatted fences over a metre high (4 ft) will be scaled on occasions.

Hedgehogs can swim fairly well and they can also squeeze through extraordinarily small holes. They seem to be such podgy animals that they could never negotiate a gap less than 3″ (10 cm) wide. It's easy to forget that much of the hedgehog's apparent bulk is in its loose-fitting skin. This is like a chunky sweater: very mobile and enclosing a comparatively slight occupant. With spines laid flat, a hedgehog can get under a shed, through a tiny hole or between the slats of a chestnut paling fence. Once into a small space it can bristle the spines and become impossible to dislodge. A lady once wrote to me saying that a hedgehog had crawled into an old Wellington boot, what should she do? I suggested she wore the other one and hopped, but in all seriousness little else was possible. The only way to get a hedgehog out of such a tight spot is to wait for it to extract itself.

These matters were most clearly demonstrated to me when I did my first 'hedgehog' radio interview for the BBC. I put the animal on the floor and concentrated on my questions and diction. Next thing – there was no sign of my co-star. It had vanished! BBC studios are not noted for their lavish furnishings or general clutter. It was a square room with fitted carpet and nowhere to hide. It took nearly 20 minutes of searching brief cases, the corridor outside and every inch of the studio before we discovered the animal wedged in the 2″ (5 cm) gap between a heavy cupboard and the wall. There was no getting the bristling blighter out, so we had to empty the cupboard and move it before recapturing my hedgehog. Doubtless that performance would have made a more interesting broadcast than whatever it was that I had actually said in my interview.

Hedgehogs out and about: how far do they travel?

If you try to follow a hedgehog to see where it goes, it isn't long before it disappears under a bush or through a fence. It's not easy to watch furtive movements in the dark anyway. So, although it may be possible to follow a hedgehog for a short time, you are unlikely to learn much about its general movements. The 'experts' have exactly the same problem, which is why so little is known about the nocturnal wanderings of hedgehogs; the practical difficulties are such that few studies have even been attempted.

The best way to follow hedgehogs at night is to use 'radio-tracking', a technique in which a miniature radio transmitter is attached to the animal so that everywhere it goes it can be traced using a direction-finding radio receiver. All sorts of animals have been radio-tracked now, but only three or four such studies have been made of British hedgehogs.

These days we often see radio-tracking studies on TV programmes, but when I started, back in the 1960s, the idea of putting radios on hedgehogs was considered highly eccentric. In fact, one of the biggest problems was to convince the Post Office that I was serious, because they have responsibility for issuing radio licences. After six months of discussion, they finally agreed; and so it was that my hedgehogs became licensed as 'testing and development stations' in accordance with the Wireless and Telegraphy Act, 1949. The licence itself ran to several pages of foolscap paper.

My radio transmitters were home made and unfortunately they had a range of only about 100 yards. More modern equipment allows hedgehogs to be located at distances 10 times greater than this. A special aerial indicates which direction the signal is coming from, allowing us to walk towards the hedgehog until we can see it. However, hedgehogs often do nothing at all for hours; so following them can be pretty boring. It can also be chilly as the frost settles or mist rises around your knees at 4 a.m. Also, wandering about in the dead of night waving around what appears to be a TV aerial is not easily explained to a squad car full of sceptical policemen.

Anyway our radio tracking studies suggest that hedgehogs travel about 1–2 miles (2–3 km) a night in areas where there is plenty of food. Males wander further than females, and both probably travel greater distances where there is less food to delay them. Two and a half miles (4 km) is probably about the furthest straight-line distance a night's wanderings would extend to. However, these estimates are based on our studies of hedgehogs living on a golf course and in the adjacent gardens. There is little to stop them wandering freely over wide areas, but elsewhere in thick woodland or built-up areas they may well travel much less. We simply don't know. The sort of precise radio-tracking necessary for studying hedgehogs is very difficult in built-up areas because walls, fences and metal objects distort the signals. Nor is it easy for the observer to move about freely, so despite the abundance of hedgehogs in suburban areas, this is one of the more difficult habitats in which to study them. Yet generalizations about hedgehogs based on studies elsewhere may not be valid in town gardens.

The normal pattern of movement consists of a slow and careful circuitous meandering in search of food, every possible place being investigated. This is then followed by a brisk walk to another likely spot where further searchings will be made. Whilst seeking food the hedgehog wanders to left and right and often in circles, so adding considerably to the total distance covered.

Most nights, the animal will end up where it started – at its daytime nest. It will remain there until dusk and then begin another night's foray. However, hedgehogs do not always return to the same nest, especially in summer. They may stay somewhere else for several days, then return to a previously used nest. At different times, the same nest may be occupied by a series of different hedgehogs, so it is difficult to say whose nest it was originally. This is how hedgehogs pick up fleas and other parasites left behind by previous visitors. Summer nests may be quite flimsy structures but may sometimes involve the collection of grass, paper, leaves and other debris to construct something resembling the hibernation nest. Much depends on the weather and the site chosen to spend the day. The use of nests in summer is reminiscent of the way climbers come and go from huts on mountainsides, except that it is very rare to find two hedgehogs occupying the same nest at once (though they often do so in captivity). During warm weather, a nest may not be built at all; the hedgehog just lies up hidden in a grass tussock or under a pile of leaves.

There is no doubt that hedgehogs know where they are going. They don't just wander at random. The repeated appearance of marked animals in our gardens shows this. People have also 'deported' marked animals from their gardens and let them go, only to see them return the next night from distances of at least a quarter of a mile (400 metres). One radio-tracked hedgehog was removed from her nest and walked that distance more or less non-stop back to her nest of young and later retraced her steps to a favourite feeding area. How she accomplished this is a mystery. Scent trails would be difficult to follow, being criss-crossed by many other animals; there were no direct paths and no obvious visual cues. Clearly hedgehogs have a good sense of direction.

By following the same hedgehogs for weeks or even months one can get an idea of how much general space they need. If all their movements are marked on a map, the total area of a male hedgehog's normal stomping grounds seems to be about 20–30 hectares (60 acres or so). Females make do with much less (10 ha). Biologists call an animal's normally used area its 'home range', but this is a fairly woolly concept, especially for hedgehogs. Some hedgehogs stay in much the same place and use a similar area from month to month or even in successive years. Others appear to be 'of no fixed abode' and wander widely and unpredictably.

People often confuse the idea of 'home range' with that of 'territory'. While

he former is a normal area of activity, territory is only that part of the area which
n animal actually defends. Birds often have territories (one robin will chase
nother from its patch of garden lawn for example) and some mammals do too.
et if you follow hedgehogs night after night, you find their paths cross and
ntermingle. None of the animals appears to defend its own patch and keep out
ther hedgehogs; they all wander freely at will. In this sense, hedgehogs do not
ave a territory; yet they often fight if they meet. It's quite likely that hedgehogs
re non-territorial by the conventional definitions, but do defend the immediate
pace around where they happen to be. Hedgehogs need elbow room, not an
mpire. Subordinate hedgehogs can use the same areas as the dominant ones, just
o long as they do so at a different time. Feral (gone-wild) cats appear to have a
milar social organization; but the details are less well known in hedgehogs
ainly because of the problems of studying small furtive creatures in the dark.

Some animals, like otters, leave their droppings as territorial signposts: animal
keep out' notices to warn off trespassers. Dogs leave their scent messages on
amp-posts. So far as we know, hedgehogs don't do these things. They leave their
roppings apparently at random and it's impossible to say where they urinate
ecause it's done so unobtrusively. Nevertheless, the hedgehog has a keen nose
nd is bound to be capable of recognizing the smell of other hedgehogs and their
roducts. Perhaps this is all they do, merely noting who is about and who has
assed by recently. This is all that is really necessary if they are not defending
rritorial areas. When you think about it, there is no real *need* for hedgehogs to
e territorial, especially in suburban areas where there is plenty of food. Why
other to waste energy defending a territory if you don't need to?

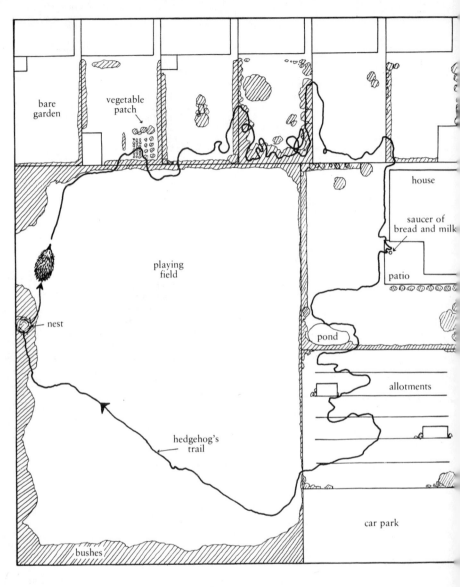

bare garden

vegetable patch

house

saucer of bread and milk

playing field

patio

nest

pond

allotments

hedgehog's trail

car park

bushes

Typical night's meanderings

Why are hedgehogs nocturnal?

The hedgehog's spines are such good protection against predators that there seems little need to be active only under cover of darkness, hence the question. We ask such a question because we presume that being active in daylight is the norm and animals doing anything else require some sort of explanation. In fact from a biological point of view, it's the other way round; nocturnal behaviour is the norm for mammals in general and has been ever since they first evolved. It's diurnality that's special.

True, the hedgehog could get away with being active in daylight, and often does; but there is no positive advantage in doing so and a serious problem. Most of the small invertebrate animals that form the natural food of the hedgehog are, for their own reasons, nocturnal. Some need to avoid daytime warmth and sunshine to cut down on their water loss by evaporation, and many benefit from moist, dew-laden night air. Most of them come out in the dark to try to avoid being seen and eaten. So the reason why hedgehogs are nocturnal is that most of their food is too and there would be no advantage in changing the habit of millions of years.

Radio hedgehog on the air

One design of radio transmitter was attached to an elastic harness, tailor-made to fit its carrier. The harness had to be elastic to allow the animal to roll up. More recent designs have been smaller and can be glued directly to the spines. The transmitter weighs less than $1/20$th of the hedgehog itself, so it is not a major encumbrance (the equivalent of a human carrying an empty rucksack). Power comes from tiny deaf-aid batteries. These can be changed by unscrewing a threaded bung in the transmitter so that the hedgehog can be fitted up with new batteries without taking its radio off.

The transmitters can be home made with a little practice and cost about £6 each to build. The direction-finding aerial is not difficult to make either. Anyone could go radio-tracking hedgehogs if it were not for problems with the receiver. The Post Office will not allow transmitters to work on radio frequencies that might interfere with the BBC or police walkie-talkies, so the hedgehog transmitters must be built to emit a higher frequency signal. In turn that means the receiver must be capable of picking up such signals and normal transistor radios can't. However, for about £50 you can get a special converter which allows a normal transistor radio of good quality to be modified to do the job. Thus a make-do, but workable radio-tracking system could be built for about £150, given a bit of patience and workshop expertise. To purchase such kit from a scientific suppliers would cost at least 3 or 4 times as much and might not work much better.

Hedgehogs in the garden

There is no doubt at all that the hedgehog is the gardener's ally. It eats countless insect pests and does no harm. There is thus every reason to give hedgehogs all the encouragement we can to get them to live in and around our gardens. Besides, they make amusing and interesting visitors to our patios on summer evenings.

Unfortunately many of us, well meaning towards hedgehogs in every other respect, don't make life easy for them at all. Indeed, without realizing it, we may easily turn our gardens into hedgehog death traps. It's silly to put out food for them only to find that they are claimed as victims of the garden pond. A survey in London suggested that nearly ten per cent of all dead hedgehogs reported had drowned: not because they can't swim but because they can't escape from some ponds. Plastic pond liners and sheer-sided swimming pools are fatal. The best way

to help hedgehogs out if they fall into these things is to have a piece of wood floating as a life raft or (much better) one or two small strips of chicken wire dangling over the edge into the water. Hedgehogs will climb these like scrambling nets and make good their escape.

A little bit of forethought will also remove another potential hedgehog hazard – tennis nets. These are often left lying on the ground as a long sausage of net, or loose netting trails on the grass. Foraging hedgehogs easily get tangled up in this stuff and will die unless noticed and rescued. Try to keep tennis nets tied up off the ground when not in use. A similar problem exists with pea and strawberry nets, though here of course we can't lift the net out of reach or the birds will get in. The solution is to peg the edges of the net down *tightly*. If the net is held taut, it is much less likely to become tangled round a hedgehog's feet and spines.

Tidy-mindedness is another problem. Gardeners like to sweep up dead leaves, root out brambles and keep their patches neat, but in doing so remove vital sites for winter nests and necessary nesting materials. Obviously few of us want a wilderness in our back yard just for the hedgehogs, but if we all keep our gardens surgically clean then the habitat becomes unsuitable for hedgehogs to live in permanently. This may be why people have hedgehogs for a few months and then lose them with the onset of winter; there is nowhere to make a sound winter nest. The solution to this problem is constructive untidiness. Leave the fallen leaves behind the shed; don't dismantle the log pile down to ground level till late in the winter; try to leave hedge bottoms alone and don't rake them out too often; leave odd corners and nooks; imagine yourself to be a hedgehog. Try also to be sparing, selective and sensible in the use of garden chemicals; remember what they do and remember that a hedgehog may see things differently to you.

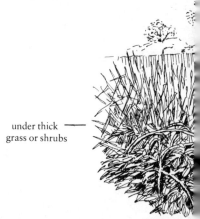

under thick
grass or shrubs

Good hibernation sites in a typical garden. Anywhere that a pile of leaves may form and remain undisturbed over winter is suitable; there is no need to build a special hedgehog house if dry secluded nooks are already available

under compost heap

behind piled logs

under pile of leaves

Putting out food for garden hedgehogs

There must be thousands and thousands of people throughout the length and breadth of Britain who put out food each night for their hedgehogs, treating them as Honorary Members of the household, free-ranging pets. I wonder how many cows work full time to produce milk for the benefit of British hedgehogs? There are plenty of soft-hearted Continental householders too, and in Germany you can even buy special packets of 'Igelfutter' (hedgehog food) in the shops.

Wild hedgehogs will readily take to bread and milk, put out each evening. Initially they will come for it late, after house lights are out. But gradually they will get bolder and will soon learn to feed close to the house with light streaming on to them from the windows. The key thing is to ensure if possible that the food bowl is either always in the dark or always well lit. Try not to have some nights with curtains open and others with them closed. This will cause hesitancy among your hedgehog visitors until they get used to your habits. But remember, the 'hogs that come to your patio may not always be the same ones, so don't be surprised if 'it' seems to be tame one night and very shy another.

Putting out grub for the 'hogs gives a lot of pleasure to a lot of people and must contribute a fair bit to the total amount of food that passes down hedgehog throats. But is it a Good Thing? What effect does all this largesse have on the hedgehog population, bearing in mind that studies on other animals show that major biological factors such as breeding success and territory size are significantly affected by food availability. Also there is the question of food suitability. Most people put out bread and milk for their hedgehogs, but could this actually be more harmful than helpful? These two major issues are explored further in the next few pages. The same hedgehogs will come night after night, year after year, to eat food put out for them. They obviously welcome it, and it is reasonable to suppose that they do not travel further than necessary to get it. Thus, if food is regularly provided in a garden, you might assume the hedgehogs take up residence nearby; and that when they leave the nest each night, they make a 'bee line' straight for the food bowl so as to arrive as soon as possible, before other hedgehogs have eaten the food. Most people I know who put out food for hedgehogs take these things for granted and further assume that 'their' hedgehogs, numbering only 2 or 3 at most, treat the garden and its precious food bowl as valuable territory and do not share these resources more than necessary with other hedgehogs.

These assumptions are so logical that they must surely be true. In which case perhaps the hedgehogs become addicted to an easy meal of bread and milk and fail to eat enough natural food to make a balanced diet? Worse still, maybe they become so dependent upon food bowls being filled each evening that when peopl go away on holiday or fail to put out food for other reasons, the hedgehogs suffer real distress? In order to investigate these ideas in some detail, my students and I carried out a radio-tracking study of hedgehogs that had already become accustomed to feeding at food bowls. The main study site was in the gardens adjacent to a golf course, the other site was my own garden. We made observations on 3 to 5 animals in an evening, recording their positions and activity every 60 seconds for up to 6 hours at a stretch. We also watched their customary food bowl from dusk till midnight. Our observations were later fed into a computer which printed a map of where the hedgehogs had been and summarized their activity for the night. We set out to answer a series of specific questions.

How close to the food bowl do the hedgehogs live?

None of the food bowl 'regulars' lived in the garden where food had been put out for years (despite apparently suitable sites being available). One lived next door in the runner bean patch for a few days, another lived 60 yards away under a garden shed, but mostly the nest sites were over 100 yards distant. Two of the hedgehogs came in from over a third of a mile (half a kilometre) away, despite the fact there were plenty of other nest sites nearer the food. In fact one of these animals moved nearer the garden for a couple of days, then went back to its remote nest. The one in the conveniently local bean patch moved too, but went to live in a thicket over three times further away from the food bowl. So hedgehogs don't appear to move into a cluster round the regular supply of food.

Altogether, about 50 hedgehogs lived on the golf course within hedgehog walking distance of our study food bowl, but probably less than one third of them actually visit the bowl in a year.

Do they wake up and make a 'bee line' for the food?

If a bowl of bread and milk were an irresistible magnet for hedgehogs, we would expect them to travel the shortest possible distance from the nest to the bowl and get there as soon as they could. In fact hardly any of the hedgehogs tried to do either. They often left the nest and set off in quite the wrong direction at first. At least half of them travelled more than twice as far as they need have done. One of them had journeyed over ¾ mile (1.2 km) before reaching the bowl which was only 200 yards away by the shortest route.

Mostly the hedgehogs took more than twice as long as they need have done to reach the food bowl. Several did not arrive for two or three hours when they could have done so in 15 minutes. Some nights they didn't bother to come at all and spent their time foraging on the golf course instead. Often the hedgehogs wasted 10 minutes or more (an hour and a half in one case) courting other hedgehogs, even though this was the end of the breeding season. A couple of the animals were prone to sitting about doing nothing for long periods, indifferent to the bread and milk which awaited them only a short distance away. In a couple of instances, hedgehogs travelled to the garden and then didn't bother to visit the bowl at all.

The hedgehogs were certainly very variable in their behaviour; they obviously pleased themselves what they did and were not behaving like robots to fit our preconceived ideas of what they should do.

Are hedgehogs 'faithful' to one garden?

Now this is going to upset a lot of folk.

In 17 nights, at least 11 different animals visited our principal food bowl. The 6 radio-tagged ones (all caught at that bowl) showed that they did not simply come in off the golf course to feed at the special bowl and then go back to eating natural food. They all went to other gardens as well. Sometimes, because of hedgehog-proof fences and walls, this necessitated a devious route in and out of garden gates and via secret hedgehog holes; but the normal pattern was to forage from one garden to the next, taking in neighbours' food bowls on the way. So each particular garden does not have its own separate set of visitors. Moreover, on some nights the animals deserted the study garden and went to visit others in another road 200 yards away.

These findings answer another question too: it is obvious that hedgehogs do not stake out a territory and defend 'their' food bowl. They might fight off another animal which sought to feed at the same time, and timid hedgehogs clearly avoided competing with others. However, even our most active and dominant male hedgehog showed no sign whatever of trying to retain exclusive rights over the garden or its food bowl.

How much bread and milk does a hedgehog eat?

We weighed the food bowl before and after each hedgehog had fed and we also noted the time it took to eat the weight of bread and milk removed. The largest amount guzzled in one go was $3\frac{1}{2}$ oz (94 g) (over 10% of the hedgehog's body weight; equivalent to one of us eating 17 lb/8 kg. of porridge). Usually the animals ate only half that amount, but they often came back later for more. One slurped its way through $5\frac{1}{2}$ oz (157 g) during the course of an evening.

Overall, the average rate of consumption was $\frac{1}{4}$ oz (7 g) per minute spent at the bowl, so it is now possible to time feeds with a watch and estimate the amount eaten by each animal by multiplying the number of minutes by $\frac{1}{4}$ oz (7 g).

Does this stop them eating enough natural food?

We can't answer this question properly because nobody knows what constitutes 'enough'. Nor have we yet got an accurate estimate of just how much natural food hedgehogs do eat in an hour or an evening (but we're working on that). However, we can be certain that none of our hedgehogs ate only bread and milk. They might like it and eat lots of it, but they also spent a lot of time in normal foraging. This is precisely why they took so long to get to the food bowl and often didn't bother to come at all; they were busy picking up natural food, either on the golf course or around the gardens. After a big meal at the bowl, a hedgehog often sat still in the shrubbery for half an hour, no doubt burping gently, but always set about natural foraging again before going back to its nest. So they don't end up abandoning a natural diet in favour of living off bread and milk alone.

What happens when the poor hedgehogs aren't fed?

We tried the experiment of not putting food in the bowl for a few nights to see if the hedgehogs would just sit in the shrubbery waiting for food or go elsewhere. Reactions differed; some went to a neighbour's bowl, one charged about as though in disbelief (but the next night, took one sniff at the empty bowl and departed immediately). Another animal came back in hopes five times in one evening. None of them just sat waiting; all went and found other food.

We tried repeating these studies in my own garden, but for a much shorter time and on only three animals. The results were similar; none lived in the garden, they did not make a bee line for the food (even once they had reached the garden) or hurry themselves; all spent most of their time in natural foraging.

So it looks as though bowls of bread and milk are a welcome supplement to the hedgehog's diet, but not the disruptive influence on sensible living that people often assume. Perhaps this isn't so surprising after all. Consider our own relationship with fish and chip shops. The food is warm, nutritious, cheap and plentiful; it's tasty too. We don't have the bother of washing up, nor do we have to cook the food ourselves. So why don't we all live next door to a chippy and eat there every night? And why isn't there widespread woe and hunger on Sundays when the chip shop is shut?

Is bread and milk a suitable food for hedgehogs?

There is not much published information about hedgehog milk. However, one analysis suggests that it is more concentrated than cow's milk, containing twice as much protein and over twice the amount of fat. So cow's milk isn't as good as hedgehog milk, but some people go further than that and suggest that cow's milk is actually harmful to hedgehogs, making them ill and causing diarrhoea.

Is this true? It's not what the 'Drinka pinta milka day' adverts say. It also overlooks the fact that all mammals depend wholly on milk for the first few weeks of their life. True, that's milk from their mother, not a cow; but there is nothing actually poisonous in cow's milk. In fact it contains an excellent mixture of sugar, fat and protein: just what animals need. What harm is done by drinking it? The diarrhoea suffered by some animals may be caused by something quite different. It is easy to settle this question by performing a simple series of experiments (see p. 76) and it appears that if there is too much milk in the diet, hedgehogs will indeed get 'the runs'. Hence it is a good idea to ensure that the diet is varied and does not consist wholly of bread and milk. It is unlikely that wild hedgehogs exist solely on this unnatural food (see p. 73), so don't worry about the nightly saucer of bread and milk, but captive ones should be given a varied diet by offering table scraps, dog food and other things.

Bread and milk is said to be fattening and, for this reason, should not be offered in large amounts to birds in the breeding season lest they stuff their nestlings with it and stunt their growth for lack of protein. However, for hedgehogs a fattening diet is exactly what they need, especially in the autumn. They must have at least a quarter of their their body weight stored as fat (the equivalent of 35 lb/16 kg) for a full-grown man), and they have only a few weeks in which to acquire it. The fat will be vital insulation and food during winter hibernation.

In summer, hedgehogs (and many other ground-feeding animals) face the problem of drought. In periods of a week or more without rain, worms especially become hard to get and so do many other invertebrates; just at a time when many young hedgehogs are leaving the nest and trying to fend for themselves. Under such circumstances extra food and drink (of *any* kind) may mean the difference between life and death. The prolonged drought of 1976 made the ground so hard and dry that the hedgehog population in my local park was almost wiped out. Yet nearby garden hedgehogs were still numerous, thanks no doubt to extra food and drink put out in bowls.

Critics argue that, given bread and milk, hedgehogs will gorge themselves to the point of discomfort. Does that really matter, we sometimes do it ourselves? It is also said that the animals will fill up on bread and milk which is a poor substitute for the natural food that they no longer feel it necessary to seek. But where is the evidence for this? Nobody knows in detail where hedgehogs go and what they do in their nocturnal rambles. Where is the evidence that a bread and milk meal affects normal foraging behaviour? In order to shed some light on this matter my students and I carried out a radio-tracking study of some hedgehogs that were known to visit gardens and eat bread and milk regularly (see p. 71).

These studies suggest that extra food of this sort does not significantly affect behaviour and merely serves as a supplement to the natural food that is gathered during the rest of the night. What we need are more studies and information of this kind so that we can actually *know* what is going on, not just guess.

Bread and milk is not ideal fodder and should never be the major part of a hedgehog's diet. It makes a valuable supplement to natural food and, in times of scarcity, finding such a dish must be very welcome indeed; perhaps even a salvation and certainly better than slow starvation. Many hedgehogs actually seem to prefer it to natural food and may often be seen guzzling bread and milk while slugs, which would normally be seized and eaten, feed alongside.

Perhaps the last word should come from the hedgehogs themselves. As I write, there are furtive scufflings in the darkness outside. Our hedgehogs are voting with their feet. They have been coming regularly for our bread and milk over the past few weeks; some were here last year too. They show no signs of tummy ache and are plump and healthy. If our bread and milk is bad for them, they are certainly gluttons for punishment.

An experiment to discover whether bread and milk causes diarrhoea in hedgehogs

We used four captive hedgehogs (3 females, 1 male) and fed them Pedigree Chum dog food diluted with crumbled dog biscuit, knowing this to be a good standard diet for hedgehogs. There was plenty of water for the animals to drink.

On this diet, the hedgehog's droppings were all firm and a dark brown colour. We then fed them only on bread and milk for ten days, and this resulted in green sloppy droppings. Back on Chum for a week and all was well again. We then tried bread and water for a few days, biscuit and water, and finally biscuit and milk. Each experimental period was separated by a short time with Chum for food. The milky diets certainly caused diarrhoea and green droppings, but this was at least partly due to excess fluid in the diet because even water mixed with bread or biscuit caused the droppings to be rather loose.

The results were the same for all four animals and it is clear that bread and milk alone is not an ideal diet. However, all four hedgehogs kept up a healthy body weight throughout the eight experimental weeks. Their weight dropped sharply over the weekends as they were not fed on Sundays, but recovered again the following week whether they were fed bread and milk or anything else.

Conclusion: bread and milk is not an ideal diet and should be varied if possible. But hedgehogs are much better off having bread and milk as a supplement to natural food than if they have to rely only on natural food.

Marking and recognizing hedgehogs

With practice it is possible to recognize small differences in the shape, size and behaviour of individual hedgehogs. However, many of them do look very much the same, especially in the dark; many people are convinced that they can recognize 'Winston, the big male' and other hoggy characters, but they may in fact be seeing more animals than they realize. The only way to be absolutely *certain* of individual identity is to mark the animals yourself. This will enable you to see how many hedgehogs visit your garden (usually more than you imagine); how often they come and how they behave towards each other.

The best way to mark hedgehogs is to put paint on their spines, using either a brush or an aerosol spray can. Quick drying paint should be used to colour a patch about 1″ (3 cm) in diameter, without matting the spines if possible and avoiding paint getting on to the hedgehog's skin or fur. White paint shows up best in torchlight; metallic touch-up paints for cars are quite suitable. You *must* avoid getting paint near the animal's face and ears.

You can paint numbers on the hedgehogs, but they are often difficult to read. It is better to use patches put on in accordance with a pre-designed code. For example, imagine the animal divided into four quadrants – right shoulder, left shoulder, right and left hip. Put one paint patch in each of these and you have four individually recognizable hedgehogs. Use pairs of patches in combination (e.g. rt shoulder + rt hip, left hip + rt shoulder, etc.) and you have 10 individual patterns. The system can be extended to accommodate larger numbers if need be,

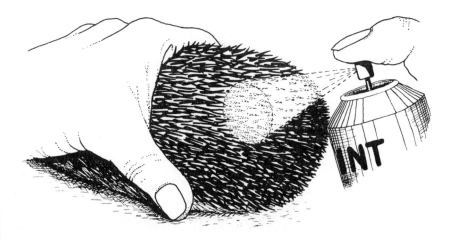

by using up to 4 patches on one animal or adding a 5th rump patch like a cottontail rabbit (see chart).

Paint marks will remain visible for up to six months, sometimes longer. However, they get dirty quickly and may need close inspection to be detected after a few weeks.

A suggested marking code—copy this out and fill in the date, sex and weight of the animal marked with each pattern as you use it. Start at no. 1 and work through.

NB *This assumes a maximum of two paint patches on any one animal. The series can be extended beyond 10 by having up to 5 patches per animal.*

Animal no.	Right shoulder	Right hip	Left shoulder	Left hip	Date 1st caught	Sex	Weight
1	X						
2		X					
3			X				
4				X			
5	X	X					
6	X		X				
7	X			X			
8		X	X				
9		X		X			
10			X	X			

Use this scheme to recognize animals and give each a name or number. Once you have a population of marked animals you can begin some really interesting studies. First of all: how many hedgehogs come to your garden? Some people think they have 1 or 2 and in fact it's 8 or 10. You can check to see whether the bold ones or the slinky ones always behave that way or only when they are alone. How long do certain individuals continue to come regularly? Do young ones stay or disperse? How do hedgehogs behave towards one another? This is a key area of interest because little research has been done on the social behaviour of wild hedgehogs, so even an amateur study at home can contribute new information (provided the observations are systematic and careful). For example, some hedgehogs will drive others away from a food bowl; but is such dominance due to body size (big always dominant over small), are males dominant over females or does a hedgehog's position in the social hierarchy depend on something else? A study of the 'peck order' among hedgehogs would be most interesting. Marked animals can be watched to see who courts with whom, who fights or runs away, who feeds first at a bowl and who hangs back in the shrubbery. If you clip patches of spines as well as using paint to mark them, your hedgehogs ought to be recognizable the following year. Then you can see whether it's the same one that returns, how long it lives and how many are marked and never seen again. In fact a large number fall into this last category, suggesting that the hedgehog population may contain a large number of nomads. That's interesting for a start, but are these in fact young animals or the ones you have observed to be subordinate in the peck order? Maybe they are just being driven out by the resident hedgehogs?

Having marked animals come to your feeding bowl vastly increases the interest of watching them (not to mention the mice that nip in to steal food and the occasional fox that comes too). Hedgehog watching on a dimly lit patio can be great fun. On most summer evenings it certainly beats watching television.

A lady in Hertfordshire has kindly sent me her hedgehog attendance register for 1982. It spans 17 weeks of the summer from mid-May. She marked the animals with different colours and writes: 'I am amazed how many there are. In fact a sudden rush of new hedgehogs causes a paint crisis!' At least 9 hedgehogs visited the food bowl. The register shows 'White' came consistently throughout the summer, though not every night; whereas 'Red Two', having discovered the food bowl in mid-July, hardly missed a single night thereafter. 'Yellow' was only ever seen twice. Perhaps most interesting are the periods of absence. Despite its regular attendance, 'White' would not be seen for intervals of 3–10 nights, even when food was available. 'Red One' came only 5 times in 3 months, with periods of 9, 12, 24 and 28 nights in between. 'Blue' was absent for up to 33 nights and 'Yellow Two' stayed away for 40 nights; all of which tends to suggest that the extra food put out for hedgehogs is very welcome but not dangerously addictive. Quite clearly the animals can manage without and frequently do so of their own free choice.

Slug pellets – are they a hazard to hedgehogs?

This is probably the question I am asked most often. It reflects a major and legitimate concern that people have for wildlife in their gardens, and their problem when trying to control damage done by slugs and snails. Because of its importance, the issue of slug pellets will be considered here in some detail. For the same reason, I also wrote to three of the biggest UK slug-pellet manufacturers asking some detailed questions. Two months later, I had not heard from one of them, another offered a bland assurance that there was nothing to worry about and they had never received any complaints. The third company offered some considered comment and referred to studies made in Switzerland by a Professor Schlatter, who seems to be the only person who has looked at this problem specifically in relation to hedgehogs.

The most important 'active ingredient' of slug pellets is a substance called metaldehyde. The reason it is used against slugs is not because it is harmless to other things, but because slugs are killed by much smaller doses of it than are other creatures. The measurement of just how poisonous it is can never be really precise because some individual animals are more resistant than others. Environmental factors also interfere; for example, the effect of metaldehyde on slugs even depends somewhat on the weather. Nevertheless, slugs are killed at dose rates between 5 and 20 micrograms of metaldehyde per gram of slug;

whereas dogs, guinea pigs and cats need 200–1000 micrograms per gram – that's 10 to 50 times as much.

In practice this means that eating, or even just contacting, a single pellet may be enough to kill a small slug; but a hedgehog sized animal, a cat or guinea pig would have to eat several hundred pellets to kill it.

That's the theory, which is based on laboratory tests to discover how much poison, per gram of animal, it takes to kill 50% of the animals eating it. But do these laboratory tests, under artificial conditions, really provide a valid basis for assuming that our garden hedgehogs are not at risk? There are still some important, explicit questions that need answering:

1. Will hedgehogs eat slug pellets?

Hedgehogs are omnivorous and will eat all sorts of things; however, they do not normally like hard dry things such as pellets, grain or stale bread. They normally prefer softer, moist food, though will have a go at almost anything. In an effort to stop birds eating slug pellets, some manufacturers incorporate a blue dye (birds have been found to peck at blue objects less often than any other colour but this is unlikely to make much difference to a nocturnal hedgehog). An unpleasant substance is also built into the pellets so that they taste and smell nasty, and this helps deter pets (and young children) from munching them in quantity. Presumably it would put the hedgehogs off too, *even* if they fancied the pellets in the first place.

2. OK, so hedgehogs probably don't eat slug pellets, but what if they eat the poisoned slugs?

Dead or sickly slugs would be easy prey for a foraging hedgehog who might readily find and consume a couple of dozen in a good night. The answer here centres on whether or not poisoned slugs have any residue of metaldehyde in or on them. Supposedly they do not. But let us imagine that a poisoned slug did contain the whole dose that caused its death (perhaps 50 micrograms for a fairly big slug): a hedgehog would need to eat about 5,000 of these to take in the sort of dose that would kill a large guinea pig and therefore (presumably) a hedgehog.

3. But aren't pesticides cumulative poisons that build up in the body? With some insecticides, tiny residues build up in the body so that although an animal never takes in a lethal dose, it goes on adding small amounts for months or years till it has finally accumulated enough to kill it. However, metaldehyde does not seem to be one of these substances. Anyway, if dead slugs contain no residues that will harm the hedgehog there should be no problem.

4. Can we be sure that results of toxicity tests using guinea pigs, rats, dogs and cats actually apply to hedgehogs too?

Hedgehogs may be more (or less?) sensitive than these laboratory animals; can we generalize from one species to another? Again we must turn to Professor Schlatter; he did test metaldehyde on hedgehogs and his results suggest that they have about the same sensitivity as cats and guinea pigs. He says it takes on average about 250 milligrams of metaldehyde to kill a 1 lb (500 g) hedgehog: an amount that no hedgehog is likely to consume.

All this seems to give a green light to slug pellets, though we might wish that the studies on hedgehogs had been repeated and corroborated by someone else.

However, this whole discussion relates to fatal doses of metaldehyde; we have not considered what effects smaller doses might have. Recent disasters in the chemical industry (e.g. with Dioxin at Seveso in Italy), fears over the widespread use of certain herbicides as defoliants in the Vietnam war, and the complaints from people living near former chemical dumps all serve to show how serious sub-lethal doses of dangerous chemicals can be. Illness, dizziness, birth defects and sterility may be caused by almost unmeasurably small amounts of harmful chemicals. Nobody can be a hundred per cent confident about the safety of hedgehogs, though on the whole it does look as though slug pellets are not as dangerous as they might be. There are plenty of other less obvious garden chemicals that just might be much worse. We simply don't know. The best advice therefore must be to use garden chemicals sparingly and only as directed, otherwise you may well be doing your hedgehogs a mischief along with your intended victims.

How to reduce the risk of hedgehogs (and other animals) eating slug pellets

1. Purchase only those that contain blue dye, to deter birds, and a substance to make them taste nasty to hedgehogs.
2. Only put them out when and where you have a slug problem.
3. Lay them inside pieces of pipe or under a low tunnel made of bricks, where hedgehogs can't get at them.
4. Remove or bury any dead slugs you find.
5. You should consider an alternative method of slug destruction (e.g. slug traps baited with beer). You could also consider using an alternative chemical to kill slugs (e.g. methiocarb), but if the manufac-

turer has not tested it on hedgehogs, you are no better off than with conventional metaldehyde pellets.

You could also think whether hedgehogs or lettuces are more important. You can buy the latter at any old greengrocers.

Finally you might remember just how often hedgehogs eat slugs and other garden pests. If, by careless use of garden chemicals you kill or debilitate your hedgehogs, your pests, having fewer predators, will rejoice and multiply and you might end up with a bigger problem than you started with.

Lifespan and survival

The first four weeks of a hedgehog's life are likely to be its last: about twenty per cent of baby hedgehogs succumb before becoming independent of their mothers. Once they have left the nest and struck out on their own, young hedgehogs are very dependent upon getting plenty of food. In dry or cold summers, this can be difficult and lead to further mortality; but in a normal year they feed well and grow steadily to reach a weight of perhaps $1\frac{1}{4}$ lb. (600 g) before it is time to hibernate in October/November. Those born early in the summer have plenty of time to do this; late-born young face serious problems (see p. 53). The next big hurdle is hibernation. Much depends upon the length and severity of winter and what fat reserves the animal was able to accumulate before winter began.

The vicissitudes of early life are such that nearly three quarters of all hedgehogs born never see their first birthday. But having survived that long, things start to look up, and the chances of surviving the next winter increase. Hedgehogs have little to fear from predators and old age doesn't begin for at least 4 or 5 years. Whereas less than one third of young hedgehogs survive into the following year, among adults the survival rate is double that; two thirds of the adults alive this year will be around next year too.

Once a hedgehog has left its mother's nest its average life expectancy is two years. Probably about four hedgehogs in a thousand might reach ten, but it must be rare indeed for any hedgehog to live longer than that.

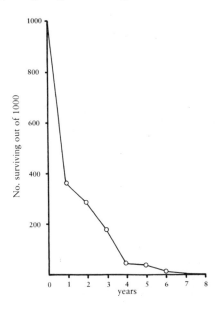

Telling the age of hedgehogs

There is no easy way of doing this, especially with live animals. Big ones are likely to be older, but size is so variable that some one-year-olds can be nearly twice the weight of others three years their senior. Some hedgehogs 'look old', but who's to know whether they are or not? The only way to be sure is to use one of the rather specialized laboratory techniques employed by biologists.

In the hedgehog it has been found that bones (especially the lower jaw) develop 'growth lines' as they get bigger, just like growth rings in a tree. The bone grows during the summer as the hedgehog is active and well fed, but in winter hibernation shuts down the processes of bone growth, interrupting its formation. By collecting jaws from dead hedgehogs and cutting thin sections of them, these alternate bands of growth and winter resting can be looked at under the microscope. The number of growth lines indicates the animal's age.

Tooth

Section of jaw bone taken for examination under the microscope

Growth lines in surface of jaw bone seen under the microscope

Causes of death

For most hedgehogs, the biggest threat to their continued survival is hibernation. At that time they are defenceless against floods, cold, disturbance and wrecking of their nests. All the time they are using up their precious and irreplaceable stores of fat which, depending on the weather, may or may not run out before foraging becomes profitable again in the spring.

Apart from these physical and physiological problems of hibernation, the hedgehog has little to fear. Whereas many small mammals run a serious risk every day of becoming food for some predator, adult hedgehogs are almost immune to attack. Badgers, polecats, even tawny owls occasionally have a go at the odd hedgehog, but they stand little chance of killing it except in the case of very young animals whose spines are thin and whose skin and rolling-up muscles are not fully developed. Bits of hedgehog are quite common in the stomachs and droppings of town-dwelling foxes, but most likely this is a result of scavenging squashed carcasses off the roads rather than deliberate killing. Foxes are supposed to push rolled-up hedgehogs into water and kill them when they uncurl. Even supposing that a fox would go to so much trouble, killing the hedgehog would still not be an easy job. Gamekeepers (see p. 99) and motor cars (see p. 102) kill some too.

Though hedgehogs are comparatively safe from enemies, they are very accident prone. They are especially good at falling into things. Perhaps this is because the cushioning effect of their spines (see p. 24) means that they do not fear falling. Anyway they fall into holes, building site trenches, rubbish pits, swimming pools and garden ponds (see p. 67) everywhere. They get caught in

cattle grids too; I heard of one where 52 had died. Recently a campaign was started in Scotland to persuade local authorities to build ramps or escape tunnels into cattle grids so that careless hedgehogs could get out. The Hedgehog Preservation Society is doing the same in England and Wales. Doubtless these escape routes will also mean a second lease of life to countless toads, newts, small mammals, beetles and lesser forms of life that might otherwise end up starved to death in the bottom of a cattle grid along with the hedgehogs.

If hedgehogs fall into cattle grids, then perhaps they also go down suburban drains? Many of these have a grille in the gutter with an adjacent hole in the kerb about 1 ft. × 6″ (30 cm × 15 cm), easily big enough to admit an inquisitive hedgehog bent on exploring the roadside. Many could die this way, though nobody has investigated whether they do or not.

Hedgehogs are at some risk from what they eat as they take a bite at almost anything within reach, some of which could be harmful to them. Very important is the fact that the things they eat most often (slugs, caterpillars, beetles, etc.) are the very things that farmers and gardeners try to kill with pesticides. It is likely that much of the hedgehog's natural food these days is contaminated with small amounts of such poisons; too little to kill its prey, but enough to slow it down so that a hedgehog is more likely to catch and eat it. One beetle may contain a minute amount of DDT for example, but the hedgehog may eat 20 of them in an hour, hundreds in a week, progressively accumulating more and more toxic substances in its own body. Who knows what effect some of these poisons might have? What we do know from studies on birds is that organochlorine pesticides (e.g. DDT, Aldrin, Dieldrin), which are specially intended for use on the sort of things hedgehogs eat, are not easily eliminated from the body. They build up slowly in the liver and in fat. Now hedgehogs depend very much on fat to tide them over the winter. By accumulating pesticide-contaminated fat during the summer a hedgehog may be sowing the seeds of its own destruction when the fat is used up during hibernation. No studies have yet been made of hedgehogs and pesticides, though one or two investigations of bats (which also feed on invertebrates and store fat for hibernation) have shown that they are very seriously threatened by pesticide contamination of their prey.

Hedgehogs are also susceptible to accidents which are not their fault. Many of them must die when gardeners burn piles of garden refuse, complete with the hedgehogs that have burrowed in to hibernate in peace over winter. Others probably get mown in the summer when long grass is cut. Certainly hedgehogs with patches of chewed-up spines are not uncommon and I have seen a three-legged hedgehog (perfectly healed and happy) which had presumably suffered such a fate. Hedgehogs also risk death through doing *silly* things, like the one seen in somebody's garage licking the acid encrustations off an old car battery.

Requiem for a Hedgehog

It wasn't cars that killed him
Or viruses or bugs.
Oh no! You thoughtless gardeners,
He ate YOUR POISONED SLUGS.

Hedgehogs as disease carriers

Hedgehogs are host to a number of viruses, bacteria and microscopic organisms which may cause serious illness in themselves or to other animals. For example, the kidneys may contain leptospires, tiny bacteria which are distributed in the urine and may cause sickness and fevers. The intestine may contain Salmonella, the bacterium which causes food poisoning. To make a list of all these potential nasties would make the hedgehog seem like a disease time-bomb, a threat to public health. However, this should be seen in perspective; most of these things have been found in other mammals at some time or other and the hedgehog is no more of a danger than any other animal.

The good news is that the hedgehog is actually less of a threat than some animals. It does not appear to be an important carrier of rabies for example, unlike the fox. It has probably played no significant role in spreading that disease across Europe in recent years and if rabies ever broke out in Britain, the hedgehog should not become a serious danger to us. Something else we can be glad about is the fact that hedgehogs have not been identified as co-villains with the badger in the spread of tuberculosis among cattle. This disease has become a serious problem in the past decade (though only in south and west England) and the campaign to gas badgers as a means of solving the problem has resulted in a lot of controversy. Hedgehogs do not appear to be important carriers of TB, though very few have actually been tested to make sure. On the other hand, hedgehogs *can* carry foot-and-mouth disease. In the event of an outbreak, it is easy to see that hedgehogs could carry this disease from one herd to another in their nocturnal rambles, despite conventional quarantine precautions. One interesting aspect of this is that experiments have demonstrated that if a foot-and-mouth infected hedgehog goes into hibernation, it will still be infective when it resumes activity the following year. Thus the hedgehog could act as a dangerous over-wintering reservoir of the disease. However, so long as foot-and-mouth is kept out of Britain, the hedgehog will not earn any black marks here.

One minor disease which I have studied in some detail is hedgehog ringworm. Ringworm is actually caused by a fungus, a bit like athelete's foot. There are several different types and they are found on the skin of various wild and domestic mammals. Occasionally humans become infected (it causes an itchy inflammation) but it's easily cured. The interesting thing is that hedgehogs have their own special kind of ringworm. It seems to do no harm, though in chronic infections the hedgehog's ears may become swollen and crusty-looking (though evidently not itchy). It was first identified among New Zealand hedgehogs and later shown to occur in Britain. With the help of Mary English at Bristol Royal Infirmary, I sampled a large number of hedgehogs (mostly road casualties) and

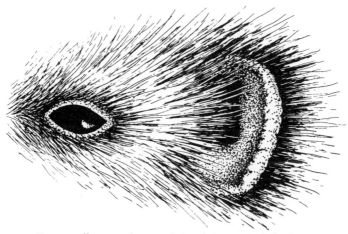

Dry, swollen ear characteristic of ringworm infection

found that one in five carried the fungus in its skin and hair roots. Males were much more often infected than females, and ringworm was found more often on the head than on the rest of the body. Urban hedgehogs were more likely to carry ringworm than those in rural areas. Our experimental efforts to transmit the fungus from one animal to another were a failure and even where it was already established, the fungus seemed to develop slowly and cause the hedgehog no harm. Hedgehog ringworm can be transmitted to humans, but it seems to be such an inefficient parasite that this rarely happens. I have never taken any precautions to avoid it (save for washing my hands after working with hedgehogs) and the fungus hasn't got to me yet. It is possible that children or others with tender skin might become infected, but not very likely.

The hedgehog does not seem to be a serious cause for concern; it comes a long way behind rats, mice and foxes as a disease carrier. This fairly rosy view needs to be qualified by adding that, as usual, few detailed studies have been made of the hedgehog in this connection, so we can't be really certain of the facts. And if some hedgehog-borne disease ever did break out, our lack of basic knowledge of this species could suddenly become a disaster.

Hibernation

There are a lot of misconceptions about hibernation. It is usually assumed to be a kind of sleep: just deeper and longer lasting than usual. Actually it's much more complex than that, and the analogy with sleep is very misleading. Hibernation is not a kind of rest or recuperation, it's an energy conservation strategy. All animals need energy, which they get from food, in order to grow, move about and live a normal active life. The hedgehog's fuel supply is in the form of worms, beetles and all the other things consumed in a night's foraging. In warm weather there is no problem, but as the weather gets colder, the invertebrates on which hedgehogs feed become scarcer and more difficult to find. If it's not careful a hedgehog may use up more energy looking for food than it can get from eating what it finds. Insectivorous birds face this problem too and many of them respond by flying away to warmer places where food is still abundant. The hedgehog can't do this and adopts the alternative strategy of becoming inactive and using as little energy as possible until the weather and food supplies improve.

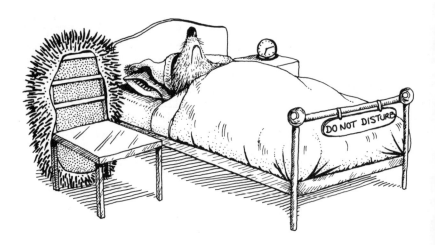

One of the most energy-expensive activities is keeping the body warm, especially for poorly insulated hedgehogs. So, to save energy, they abandon the attempt: the body furnaces are allowed to burn out and the hedgehog's temperature falls from about 35°C to 10°C or less to match its surroundings. In very cold conditions, the furnaces are stoked up gently so as to ensure that the body does not cool below 1°C and risk frostbite or freezing solid.

Allowing the body to cool saves a lot of energy, but in consequence all the chemical reactions associated with normal activities like nerve conduction,

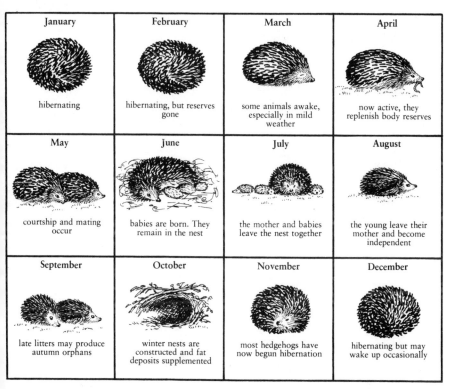

January	February	March	April
hibernating	hibernating, but reserves gone	some animals awake, especially in mild weather	now active, they replenish body reserves

May	June	July	August
courtship and mating occur	babies are born. They remain in the nest	the mother and babies leave the nest together	the young leave their mother and become independent

September	October	November	December
late litters may produce autumn orphans	winter nests are constructed and fat deposits supplemented	most hedgehogs have now begun hibernation	hibernating but may wake up occasionally

The hedgehog year

digestion, growth, breathing and movement are slowed right down almost to a standstill. The heart rate slows to less than 20 beats per minute; respiration almost stops altogether and several minutes may elapse between breaths. These changes economize further on energy expenditure, but at the price of complete immobility and major changes in the chemistry of the body which cannot be swiftly reversed.

So, faced with insufficient food/energy to maintain normal levels of its bodily activities the hedgehog responds by giving up normal activity and shutting down energy consumption to the barest minimum needed to stay alive (about 1/50th of normal requirements). This is hibernation.

Once you can understand how hibernation serves to save energy during the winter shortage of food, several worrying questions begin to answer themselves. For example, if there is plenty of food about despite it being winter, there is no *need* to hibernate (see box) and so many hedgehogs may remain active well into November and December in good years. In the warmer climate of New Zealand, hibernation is necessary for only a brief few weeks in mid-winter whereas in Scandinavia the winters are longer and so hibernation is prolonged. Conversely a period of bad weather in spring or autumn may again reduce food availability to the point where inactivity and fasting is more efficient than trying to maintain normal activity; so again hibernation may occur even though it is not winter. Hibernation is thus a flexible strategy which can be adjusted to meet different circumstances.

Perhaps you can also see why a hibernating hedgehog should *not* be kept warm? Higher temperatures (e.g. 20°C) raise the rate at which chemical reactions take place in the body and this uses up precious energy which can't be replaced without full arousal and going out to feed. Once the hedgehog has become inactive and started to hibernate, its body temperature needs to be as low as possible (a mimimum of 1°C) to slow its metabolism and the rate at which energy is used up.

Hedgehogs do come out in winter, though not very often

During hibernation the hedgehog is torpid and incapable of feeding. Its fuel supply comes from the masses of fat stored below the skin and inside its body. This is 'white fat', like you get on bacon, and at the beginning of hibernation may comprise one third of the total body weight. This precious store is gently used up over the course of the winter. In addition, there are large orange coloured lobes around the shoulders, below the skin, and these are the so-called 'brown fat'. Its special purpose is to generate heat when the animal wants to warm up and resume normal activity: fuel for the furnaces. It follows that, before it hibernates, the hedgehog must have accumulated enough white fat to last it for many weeks and enough brown fat to enable it to successfully wake up several times – otherwise hibernation will simply be a prelude to death (as it is in many young and underfed animals). So it is *vital* that hedgehogs get enough to eat in the weeks before hibernation not only to live and grow but also to store as fat to last the winter. Any baby or undersized hedgehog that hibernates at a body weight less than about 1 lb (450 g) has too little fat on board to survive more than the briefest period of winter (see p. 53).

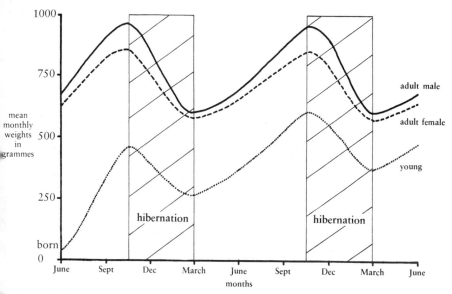

1000

750

mean
monthly
weights   500
in
grammes

250

born
0

June   Sept   Dec   March   June   Sept   Dec   March   June

months

hibernation   hibernation

adult male

adult female

young

Body weight drops over winter as fat reserves are used up and rises as they are replenished in summer

It is generally assumed that hibernation is continuous – that all being well, the hedgehog goes to sleep about Guy Fawkes day and wakes up at Easter. In fact arousal is both normal and fairly frequent. On average, hedgehogs wake up about once a week, though some may not do so for 3 or 4 months. Arousal involves raising the body temperature from perhaps 5°C to 30°C or more and this usually takes at least 3–4 hours. The hedgehog then spends a day or two in a fairly normal state before sinking back into hibernation. During this time the hedgehog may leave its nest and go for a walk, but this is comparatively rare. The majority of these arousal periods are passed inside the nest. This periodic wakefulness happens quite spontaneously, though of course hedgehogs will also be aroused by disturbance, flooding and even unseasonably warm sunshine.

There have been many studies made on hedgehogs in the laboratory (particularly by researchers in Scandinavia) to discover the physiological details of hibernation, but hardly anything is known about hibernation habits in the wild. To remedy this, I studied the hedgehogs in a West London park for six winters, recording when and where the nests (hibernacula) were built, how often they were used and how long they lasted. As the autumn nights got colder, the hedgehogs stopped using the main grassy areas of the park and began to congregate inside small (supposedly rabbit proof) fenced-off areas of brambles and scrub. Here they built their winter nests, tucked up against fallen logs or underneath bramble strands or piles of brushwood. Elsewhere they use similar sites and also go under sheds and even down rabbit holes to spend the winter.

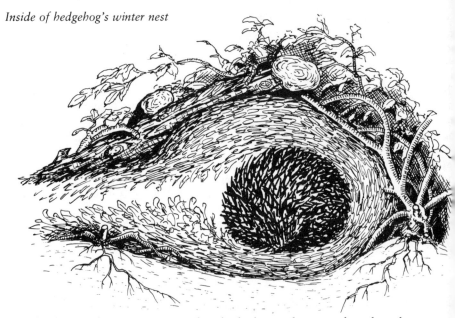

Inside of hedgehog's winter nest

There were always more nests than hedgehogs, almost as though each one built himself a spare hibernaculum in case he needed it later. Yet if a hedgehog did change nests in the middle of the winter (most did so at least once), it always built a new one and never moved into a ready-made nest. Some nests were small and soon fell to pieces. These were probably made by young animals; building good nests needs practice. Only young ones ever shared nests and then not for long; wild hedgehogs hibernate alone. Curiously they do the opposite in captivity and often insist on sharing nest boxes when others nearby remain empty.

A typical hibernation nest is a bulky structure about 20" (50 cm) in diameter, built on the ground and mostly made of leaves. Often grass, bracken and other materials are used, but leaves are best because they are more weatherproof. The hedgehog gathers them, a few at a time, and carries them in its mouth back to the chosen site. It then makes a pile, thrusting each new batch into the centre of the heap. When it has enough, the hedgehog burrows inside and begins to shuffle round and round. Normally this would simply cause the leaves to become scattered, but the site is chosen well so that the pile of leaves is held together by the support of adjacent logs or brambles. The shuffling action causes all the leaves to become similarly orientated and packed flat against each other. The nest ends up as a small chamber, entered by a short tunnel and with walls made of a wad of flat-packed leaves up to 4" (10 cm) thick. This type of nest will last well over a year, but those built one winter are never used the next winter, even when they are still available; however, other things such as bees, wasps and woodmice are eager to take them over.

The leafy hibernacula are not only very weatherproof but also provide excellent insulation against the cold (and also inconveniently warm days). In fact the nest walls are so effective that for more than three quarters of the time, the inside of the nest is kept between 1°C and 5°C, even when the air temperature falls to −8° or rises above +10°. Laboratory studies show that the hedgehog's hibernation is most efficient at conserving energy if the body is at 4°C. So the nest, the hedgehog's only protection in winter, is also playing its part in ensuring the success of the hibernation strategy. The winter nest is *so* important for the success and survival of hedgehogs that the availability of suitable nest sites and building materials may be one of the major factors which determine hedgehog distribution. Perhaps this is why they are scarce on moorland and in pine woods and marshland (see p. 16), rather than shortage of food, as is often imagined. These are the very habitats in which dry leaves are difficult to get in sufficient quantity to build a nest. Similarly, across Northern Europe, the hedgehog is rarely found beyond the limits of deciduous trees: not because it's too cold or there is no food, but simply because no trees means no leaves and no protective, insulating nest.

Baby hedgehogs in the autumn: is it cruel to take them indoors and should they be left alone?

If they have insufficient fat reserves, indicated by a body weight of less than 1 lb (450 g), leaving them alone is to condemn them to almost certain death. Indoors they can be properly fed and will remain fully active, provided that they can be given plenty of food and are not exposed to temperatures lower than about 10°C. They can then grow to a 'safe' size and be released at any time during good weather to build a winter nest and hibernate. Or, they can be kept indoors, fully fed and active all winter and be released all the better for it next spring.

NB This only really applies to babies found after about mid-September. Earlier in the summer they ought to be able to fend for themselves and are probably better off left to do so.

Is it harmful for a hedgehog not to hibernate?

No. Whereas it certainly is harmful to do without sleep, hibernation is optional. Provided there is enough food available and the air temperature is not too low (less than about 8–10°C), there is no need for a hedgehog to hibernate, so it won't. This particularly applies to hedgehogs kept indoors over winter. When they are let go in the spring, they are well fed and have a distinct advantage over wild ones whose reserves are depleted by hibernation. If kept indoors, they show no ill effects, and may go on to breed perfectly normally.

Population size and density: how many hedgehogs are there?

This question is almost impossible to answer. The problem lies with counting methods. Big animals, like deer, visible in daylight can be counted just by looking at them, perhaps aided by binoculars. But hedgehogs are nocturnal and hard to see in the dark even out in the open; who knows how many more of them lurk under bushes and in long grass and dense woodland?

Biologists often use 'mark and recapture' methods to census animal populations. A sample of animals is caught, marked and released. Later another sample is caught, and from the proportion of marked to unmarked animals in the second sample an estimate is made of total population size. It's fine with beetles and even mice, but not hedgehogs. You can't catch big enough samples at once, nor be sure that your catching method is not itself interfering with the population.

People can mark the hedgehogs that visit their gardens. Suppose that 10 animals show up in the course of a month. Does that mean that every garden has 10 hedgehogs? How many of those 10 are also part of the 10 that visit someone else's garden? What about the 3 that were marked and never seen again – are they dead or have they merely gone somewhere else? It's hard to say.

It has been suggested that hedgehogs live at a density of about 1 per acre (25 per 10 hectares). If the area of England is 50,000 square miles, then the English population of hedgehogs numbers about 32 million – or so the argument runs. But if the original estimate of 1 per acre was based upon seeing about 30 hedgehogs during an evening stroll through 30 acres of parkland (with plenty of scope for counting some animals twice and no allowance for family groups increasing the density) then the 'count' could be highly inaccurate. On a different evening's stroll, perhaps only 10 hedgehogs would be seen in the same area; especially if the night was cool. Of course it is also misleading to assume that the population density in one place or habitat (a park in this instance) is the same as would be found in central Birmingham or on the Pennine Way! An estimate of 32 million English hedgehogs could easily be wrong by the odd 25 million animals!

Radio-tracking studies (see p. 62) show that *on average* a hedgehog's home range might be about 50 acres (20 hectares), but it does not defend this patch as an exclusive territory; other hedgehogs share it too. Thus you can't say each hedgehog needs 50 acres, so England has 50,000 square miles ÷ 50 acres = 640,000 hedgehogs.

The best we can do for the moment is to refer to one (and only one) area that has been studied in detail. This is a West London golf course of about 100 acres (40 ha.) on which the permanent hedgehog population, according to different census methods, was about 30 animals 3 years running. This is an average density of very roughly 1 per hectare or 1 per 3 acres. However, it would be rash to use this figure to estimate the total British (or even English) population, because a golf course hardly constitutes a typical area of countryside. More studies are needed to estimate population densities in different habitats, but they will not be easy to carry out.

Are hedgehogs increasing or declining in numbers?

Until we can find some way of making an accurate hedgehog census, this question can never be answered. Since it is so difficult to estimate the size of hedgehog populations at one time, it is hopeless to compare estimates made at different times to check for increase or decrease.

The fact that we normally see hedgehogs in twos and threes rather than dozens adds to the problem. Suppose one week you have 3 hedgehogs visiting the garden; if a fourth appears the next week that's a thirty per cent increase in numbers of hedgehog visitors. But it hardly represents a thirty per cent population explosion.

Usually people ask about a decline in numbers because they have seen so many dead hedgehogs squashed on the roads. But dead hedgehogs may be a good sign as well as a bad one; a point discussed elsewhere (see p. 103).

Probably the best we can say about hedgehog population trends is that certain changes in the countryside must reduce their numbers. Conversion of huge areas from pastureland to arable crop farming depletes hedgehog numbers for two reasons. Firstly, fields of crops are treated with chemicals to kill the beetles, worms, slugs and other invertebrates that would otherwise have been the hedgehog's main food. Secondly, removal of hedgerows, copses and odd patches of waste ground to increase the ease and efficiency of arable farming deprives hedgehogs of vital winter nest sites. These changes have occurred over very big areas of our countryside in the past 20 or 30 years.

On the other hand, the expansion of towns is probably less of a threat to hedgehogs than to most animals. Food and nest sites abound in suburbia where hedgehogs are safe from gamekeepers and farmers.

Persecution by gamekeepers

There is no doubt that hedgehogs do occasionally eat the eggs and chicks of ground-nesting birds and in parts of Britain where pheasants and partridges are highly regarded such depredations constitute a capital offence. So hedgehogs and other suspected nest robbers are exterminated with an almost crusading enthusiasm. Gamekeepers see 'vermin control' as an important aspect of their job and, in the past anyway, have been encouraged in their destructive vendettas by the payment of a bounty for every predator killed. The usual reward for a hedgehog snout or tail was about threepence; a useful source of petty cash for the gamekeeper.

Nowadays, British gamekeepers are fewer in number and too busy with all sorts of other work to bother much about hedgehogs; but even so at least 5,000 (and perhaps as many as 10,000) hedgehogs are probably killed by them each year in this country. Legal protection for the hedgehog (see p. 109) may reduce this number somewhat in the future, but the gamekeeper remains one of the hedgehog's few persistent predators. On just one estate in East Anglia, nearly 20,000 hedgehogs were killed in a half a century, including 780 in a single year. Yet after 50 years an annual toll of 300 or so was still possible; there was no sign that the hedgehog was becoming extinct. The keepers said that they had managed to eradicate hedgehogs over the main part of the estate and they were simply killing immigrants that came in from surrounding farms each year. This may have been true to some extent, but many of their 'new' animals were in fact quite old, suggesting that they had escaped death for some years.

But are hedgehogs really so much of a threat to the gamekeepers' interests? The hedgehog's diet does include eggs (see p. 44), but not often. Back in the 1930s a study was made of partridge nests to see who were the major predators responsible for the destruction of over 1,200 clutches of eggs. Hedgehogs accounted for only 1.3%; foxes took 34% and were obviously the principal culprits. Moreover, cats and dogs destroyed more of the nests than did hedgehogs and nearly a third of the partridge clutches were lost because of careless farm workers driving farm machinery over them. So, if gamekeepers really want to protect partridges, they would be better off shooting farm workers not hedgehogs.

For a gamekeeper to go out deliberately trying to catch hedgehogs just to prevent a 2% loss of eggs is clearly a silly way to waste time. But actually the keepers normally do not trap specifically for hedgehogs. They set traps primarily to catch rats, weasels and stoats and simply kill hedgehogs as a kind of by-product of this activity. Nevertheless, it cannot really be cost-effective. If a keeper wants 100 more birds, the easiest way to get them is to buy some eggs from a bulk supplier and hatch them in an incubator, not go around trying to stop predators taking birds from his stock.

Modern gamekeepers are more enlightened than their forbears and do not really constitute a serious threat to the survival of hedgehogs. Indeed if we look at the changing distribution and abundance of gamekeepers over the past few decades, it seems pretty clear that they are heading for extinction sooner than hedgehogs.

Do gamekeepers reveal hedgehog population cycles?

Many big country estates keep a record of how many hedgehogs and other 'vermin' are killed on their land each year. Sometimes these records go back for decades. Some biologists have attempted to plot the numbers on graph paper to see if there are regular peaks and troughs in the totals which might suggest that hedgehog populations undergo regular cycles, with abnormally large numbers every 4 or 7 years for example. The trouble with this sort of exercise is that you can't be sure that the trapping effort has remained constant — usually it hasn't. During the wars for example, many gamekeepers were away killing real enemies instead of hedgehogs, so 'lows' in say 1916 or 1943 are meaningless. Similarly, higher numbers may be killed one year simply because an extra gamekeeper has been put on the payroll.

If you look at the numbers that gamekeepers kill each month, there is further evidence that the figures reveal 'gamekeeper effort' as much as hedgehog population size. There is often a persecution peak in May – June. One estate I visited killed large numbers in June and I protested that this was the wrong time; to eradicate hedgehogs the effort to kill them should be made before breeding not afterwards. The old gamekeeper listened to this sagely and said, 'Ah, but it's in June the varmints do the damage.' Apparently if he discovered hedgehogs any other time of the year, when clearing brushwood in the autumn for example, he would gently move them to a safer place!

Road deaths

Sadly, most of us are more likely to see hedgehogs as squashed remains on the road than as live animals amiably trundling about their business. Sometimes it is very disturbing to return from a journey by car with a distinct impression of having seen dozens of dead hedgehogs; but probably because their corpses are large and distinctive, we are just more conscious of them than we are of, say, dead rats.

The spiny skin is surprisingly resistant to repeated battering by vehicle tyres (it may even strike back on thin tyres as cyclists know to their cost). When pounded into the road, the skin remains visible and recognizable for longer than the thin

'Why did the hedgehog cross the road.
'To see its flat mate'

ft skin of rabbits and other mammals. This helps to exaggerate the apparent
bundance of road-death hedgehogs. On a car journey you may see, say, 5 rabbits
nd 10 hedgehogs, but the rabbits are likely to have been killed in the preceding
w days, whereas some of the hedgehogs will have been there for weeks.

When surveys have been carried out to discover what species are killed on the
ads most often, the poor old hedgehog usually comes in the top four mammal
ecies (along with rabbit, squirrel and brown rat). It is impossible to know, or
ven guess how many hedgehogs are killed on our roads each year, but the total
ust be in the tens of thousands. In Denmark, a country about a third the size of
ngland, surveys suggest about 70,000–100,000 hedgehogs are run over annually
ut of a total of about 10 million vertebrate animals killed). Nobody has lately
tempted an overall estimate for Britain, but one study in Hampshire recorded
12 hedgehogs in 2 years, an average of between 1 and 2 per 100 miles examined
uring the summer months. Another study in Yorkshire totted up 756 hedgehogs
5½ years: all killed within a 15-mile radius of Scarborough.

Naturally, all these dead hedgehogs cause considerable concern. Surely if the
arnage continues, hedgehogs will soon become rare or even extinct – or so say
e pessimists anyway? I would prefer to look on the brighter side and observe
at hedgehogs aren't extinct (or even particularly rare) *despite* all the road
aths, and that just shows what a prolific and successful creature the hedgehog
. It survives in spite of all this destruction. The slaughter on the roads is cause for
timism and faith in the hedgehog's resilience; not evidence of its imminent
om. It's a pity just the same that so many are killed in this way.

Despite the numbers killed, roads probably don't represent a really major
reat to hedgehogs overall. For example, of the 80 or so hedgehogs marked in
e of our study areas we only found a couple of them killed on nearby roads,
en though local traffic was very dense and very fast. A similar study in New
ealand, again in an area of high traffic density, found only four per cent of
arked hedgehogs ended up squashed on the road.

Squashed hedgehogs are probably one of the main subjects that people talk to
e about and it is very interesting to see how interpretations differ. One sort of
mment will be along the lines of, 'Hedgehogs must be getting more common,
ve seen so many more killed on the roads this year.' Another version of this is,
ve seen so many hedgehogs dead this year there can't be many left; they *must* be
tting scarcer.' The same observation, but two completely different
terpretations. There is also a third sort of comment to the effect that, 'I've seen
wer squashed hedgehogs this year; they must be getting quite scarce;' and this
servation will refer to the same year that other people claim to have seen *more*
ad animals. It serves to underline the problems of trying to estimate hedgehog
pulation sizes (see p. 96) and suggests that we can't learn anything very useful
om a study of road casualty figures. Actually we can learn something; for
ample, if you travel the same route regularly and note where hedgehogs occur,
ere do seem to be 'accident black spots' where animals are often seen dead; yet
r long distances in either direction there are few if any road casualties. Could

this be evidence that hedgehogs have regularly used trails and tend to use the same crossing points when attempting to get across the road?

Driving about we also become aware that hedgehogs are often killed near buildings and in suburban areas; fewer are seen out in open country. This is part of the evidence which suggests that hedgehog populations in some habitats (especially towns) are denser than elsewhere. Similar evidence indicates that hedgehog populations in parts of New Zealand may be denser than in Britain. There are simply more animals killed on a given length of road there than here. In this case we are making the assumption (perhaps wrongly) that the number of dead hedgehogs is a reflection of the number of live ones. In other words, when there are more hedgehogs out and about, more will end up dead on the roads. Carrying this assumption further, we can compare numbers seen at different times of the year; the frequency of road casualties is then a kind of barometer to indicate the level of general hedgehog activity through the seasons.

The problem with trying to analyse road casualty figures is that you are studying not just hedgehogs but traffic too. The summer months bring out the motorists as well as the hedgehogs, and some of the increased numbers of corpses seen may simply be because there is more traffic about, so more deaths occur. Fine weather tempts people to go out more, so there are more observations of hedgehogs made. In other words, even if hedgehogs were equally active all year round, we would still get more killed in summer and more sightings of them at that time.

The hedgehog's revenge

One interesting observation is that larger numbers are killed in April – May than in June. It has been suggested that this is due to young, inexperienced babies leaving the nest and getting run over soon after. But this can't really be the explanation because few babies leave the nest before July. Anyway the squashed hedgehogs early in the year are practically all adults. It's more likely that the peak numbers of road deaths are a reflection of greater hedgehog activity in the breeding season; more chasing about seeking mates, for example. This is especially likely to be the real explanation because about two thirds of springtime road casualties are males.

SPRING

adults – sex ratio 1.9:1

66% males	34% females

AUTUMN

first summer animals (young of the year) – sex ratio 1:1.2

46% males	54% females

adults – sex ratio 1:3

25% males	75% females

The sex ratio in samples of hedgehogs collected from roads varies with the time of year

Running hedgehogs: evolution in action?

The reason that the hedgehog comes a cropper so often is of course due to the animal's natural reaction to danger. If attacked, it rolls up; excellent protection against predators but no defence in the face of 10-ton lorries. Some years ago, a theory was given wide publicity that hedgehogs may be evolving into a new form that runs away from oncoming traffic instead of rolling up and staying put. The idea had a convincing air

of Darwinian natural selection: 'survival of the fittest'. Hedgehogs that rolled up when threatened by approaching vehicles got squashed and eliminated from the population. Those that ran away instead lived to see another day and pass on their 'running' genes to the next generation of hedgehogs. Thus, the theory ran, we are witnessing the evolution of a new race: the fleet-of-foot hedgehog.

The idea has a convincing simplicity about it; it may even be right, though there is no way of testing it because we can't compare the behaviour of modern hedgehogs with their behaviour in the years before cars were invented. The main trouble with the theory is that it is based on a false assumption— that running away increases the probability of escape. It doesn't (see diagram). Running could, in some circumstances, be more dangerous not less. The only way that running could really help is if the hedgehog could run faster than the approaching vehicle. This can't happen often even though some hedgehogs can travel quite fast and some drivers move extraordinarily slowly.

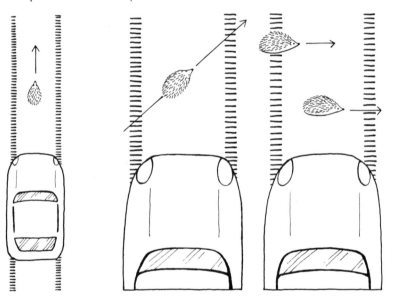

A. If the hedgehog runs in the same direction as the car, it is either still in or still out of the path of the wheels.

B. If the hedgehog runs obliquely across the path of the car it spends longer in the wheel tracks though crossing them at an angle – therefore more likely to be killed, not less.

C 1. The only way running will help escape is if the animal is already in the wheel path and it runs at right angles to the car's path, getting it out of the way. But it mustn't run under the other wheel, and is best off doing a U turn – which takes longer and therefore still involves the risk of being run over.

C 2. If the hedgehog is in the path of the car, but not actually in the track of the wheels, it is better off staying still. To run means going into the path of the wheel and risking death.

In short, running doesn't guarantee survival, nor even improve the chance of it.

Hedgehogs and the law

In 1566, in the reign of Queen Elizabeth I, a law was passed for the 'Preservation of Grayne'. This listed various animals (like rats and mice) that were thought to be responsible for damage to agricultural interests, declared them to be vermin and put a price on their heads to encourage wholesale destruction. For some reason, the hedgehog was fingered as a villain and it was decreed that payment of threepence should be made for every hedgehog killed throughout the realm. Churchwardens were charged with the duty of paying out this money for all the hedgehogs and other vermin slaughtered within their parish. They did so, and meticulously recorded these bounty payments in the parish records.

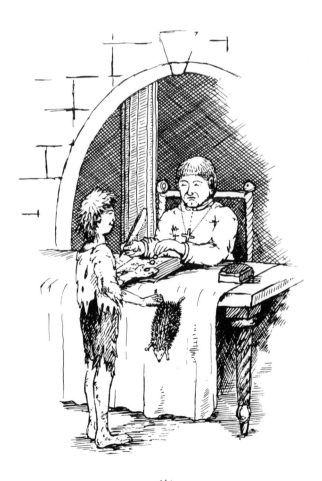

Today, in county record offices, it is possible to inspect the old churchwardens' accounts, painstakingly inscribed with quill pens in big ledgers, recording the fate of thousands of hedgehogs in bygone years. Sometimes the records continue for decades, reflecting diligent persecution. In other places, the killing of hedgehogs was more desultory. Where a long series of records exist, we can plot the number killed per year on a graph and sometimes get a result that looks like evidence of population cycles in the hedgehog. However, we should not jump to hasty conclusions for the same reason that applies to the interpretation of gamekeeper's records (see p. 101). We do not know for sure that the effort put into catching hedgehogs was the same from year to year. Far from having cycles of abundance, the hedgehog population might have been stable and the fluctuations in numbers killed recorded by churchwardens may only reflect different levels of blood-thirstiness in successive generations of parishioners. An even more likely cause for these annual variations would be the periodic rediscovery by impecunious little boys that their local churchwarden was a useful source of extra pocket money to be gained at the expense of a few hapless hedgehogs.

It is clear that nobody went all-out to eradicate hedgehogs, despite bounty payments. Indeed, with the benefit of hindsight, we can see today that bounty payments are an ineffective method of pest control. Modern experience with foxes, squirrels and other animals with an official price on their heads suggests that the 'vermin' often end up more abundant than before and country folk treat their vermin populations not as pests, but as a valuable economic resource.

Bounty payments certainly don't seem to have caused the extinction of hedgehogs, but when I first learned of them I thought it would be amusing to take a couple of dead hedgehogs to my local parish officials and demand the payment due to me under that statute of Elizabeth I. However, I quickly discovered that the law in question had been repealed in 1863, along with a whole batch of other obsolete and useless legislation; the hedgehog is officially blameless once again.

For 300 years the hedgehog was, by Act of Parliament, a statutory pest. Ironically, it is today, also by law, a protected animal. The Wildlife and Countryside Act of 1981 sought to harmonize British legislation with that of other European countries. The result was a complex hotch-potch that may take years to sort out and fully implement. The hedgehog is not one of the mammals given absolute protection (like the otter for example), but is listed (in Schedule VI) along with the red squirrel and certain others as animals that may not be captured or killed by certain methods without a licence. Another list explains what the 'certain methods' are. Literally interpreted, our new countryside legislation makes it illegal to kill hedgehogs using a machine gun and also, more inconveniently, it is now illegal for anyone to pick up a hedgehog at night using a torch without an official government licence. Clearly this wasn't really the intention of the Act, but that's how it comes out on paper. Laws ought to mean what they say and they ought to be obeyed; but in this case literal interpretation borders on the farcical. Hedgehogs may not be trapped either, except under special licence, and this creates a problem for gamekeepers who often catch hedgehogs as a by-product of trapping for something else.

The first Queen Elizabeth declared hedgehogs to be vermin, but the second Queen Elizabeth has now made them a protected species. History may reveal that neither made much difference; the evidence for hedgehogs really being vermin is as debatable as the need for present-day protection. Modern hedgehogs are not a threatened species, or at least not threatened by the sort of things the law now seeks to stop. The main reason why hedgehogs are on the list of protected species is probably that this brings Britain into line with some other European countries where, as a matter of principle, animals are protected automatically unless they are actually a pest. Legal protection will not save hedgehogs from being squashed on the roads, nor will it eliminate the effects of garden chemicals. What it has done is to generate a fair bit of confusion and a whole lot of unnecessary paperwork.

The uses of hedgehogs

One of the best known uses for hedgehogs is as croquet balls by Alice in Wonderland. Alice had a lot of bother with them getting stuck in furrows. They also kept running away; though these difficulties were nothing compared to using flamingos as the mallets, with all the players fighting to get at the hedgehogs at once and the Red Queen rapidly losing her temper with the whole game.

The other well known (perhaps more practical) use for hedgehogs is as a tasty meal. In the past at least, gypsies dined off them regularly and particularly favoured animals caught in the autumn when they were very fat and juicy before hibernation. The traditional recipe called for a large dollop of clay with which to encase the hedgehog. It would then be roasted in the embers of a hot fire for an hour or two and when the clay covering was cracked off the spines would be removed too, embedded in it. I have never tried this, for the same reasons that I expect most modern gypsies haven't either. Moreover, I suspect that corned beef in tins is both more convenient and more attractive than hedgehog in clay.

Alice's use of hedgehogs

Back in the Middle Ages, many animals (including some quite repulsive ones) were believed to be useful for medicinal purposes. The hedgehog was no exception and in 1658 Topsel listed in his *History of Four Footed Beasts and Serpents* some of the ways in which potions containing bits of hedgehog were supposed to alleviate human ailments. For example, the dried rib skin, mixed with pepper and laurel leaves, cast into 3 cups of warm water was recommended for 'one that hath the colick'. Hedgehog ashes(!) were good for boils and the powdered skin would stop your hair falling out. Using burning hedgehog as a fumigant, 'by God's help', would cure urinary stones. The hedgehog's right eye, fried in linseed oil and drunk from a brass vessel would improve night vision; and its fat 'stayeth the flux of the bowels'. Today we might have more confidence in other remedies, but Topsel was only repeating what earlier authors had asserted and did not record contemporary endorsement or scepticism.

One amusing quirk is that Topsel suggested the use of hedgehogs to cure leprosy and very recently hedgehogs have indeed been used for that purpose, though not in a way that Topsel might have foreseen. It turns out that hedgehogs and armadillos are, for some reason, very susceptible to leprosy and so could make ideal animals to use in laboratory studies aimed at seeking a cure for this disease. Armadillos are not easy to get in large numbers (especially in Britain), and so hedgehogs may one day have a future as a laboratory tool in this area of medical research.

Another quite different area of medical research has a hedgehog dimension. Studies on these and other relevant animals have shown that during hibernation the body tissues are much more tolerant of trauma than is normally the case. Moreover, at reduced body temperatures, body tissues need less oxygen. These principles are put to use during major surgery, when operations on humans are carried out at artificially low body temperatures. Maybe if we understood more about the natural mechanisms of hibernation, we could go further and do without anaesthetics; or consider operations that might last for days; or 'hibernate' sick people so that they don't get any worse while they wait their turn for an operation or hospital bed? It has also been suggested that if we could find a way to make people capable of hibernating like the hedgehog, so that they would use no food and little oxygen for months at a time, it would greatly ease the problems of long-duration space travel in necessarily small space capsules. A return trip to another planet for example might take a couple of very boring years. In that time an astronaut would need a very large store of food (and get pretty fed up with it). Much better to hibernate for 6 months or so. Moreover, studies on hibernating animals suggest that they might be, to some extent, less susceptible to the damaging effects of radiation: another potentially valuable asset in space travel.

There are plenty of more prosaic uses for hedgehogs, or at least their spines. If the spiny part of the skin is stretched flat and allowed to dry hard, it forms a durable pad of sharp spikes like a bed of fine nails. In bygone days this formed the basis for the tools used for 'carding' wool and dressing flax, combing the fibres out till they lie parallel with each other as a necessary preparation for spinning into threads. A similar dried, bristly hedgehog skin made a good (if rather fierce) brush for fluffing up woollen garments and combing out tangles in woollen cloth.

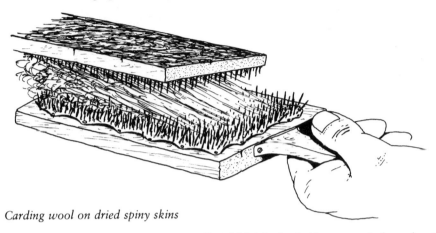

Carding wool on dried spiny skins

On a live hedgehog, the spines will yield fairly freely if you touch them, but in a dried skin they are fixed rigidly. A mass of such spines is a potential hazard, worse than a barbed wire carpet, and an effective deterrent to casual contact. Small wonder that in days gone by, farmers would nail hedgehog skins to the top rail of their orchard gates to keep out small boys. It is also said that nineteenth-century coachmen attached hedgehog skins to strategic parts of their carriage shafts to prevent their horses from dozing on the job. If the weary horse leant to one side for a snooze in the shafts, it got an uncomfortable jab in the haunches to keep it awake.

Hedgehogs in folklore: carrying apples

One of the oldest stories about hedgehogs must be the one about carrying fruit on their spines. This activity was described by Topsel in his *History of Four Footed Beasts and Serpents* and is mentioned in almost all the English accounts of hedgehogs published in the 300 years since then. Topsel probably got the tale from the works of the Roman author Pliny who had written down a mixture of fact and fable he gleaned 2,000 years ago.

Hedgehogs carrying apples as depicted in 13th century drawing

Basically the story is that hedgehogs use their prickles to impale fruit and then carry it off to their nests. The fetching and carrying of apples by this means is convincingly illustrated in several mediaeval books. Sometimes the tale is embellished by having the hedgehogs climb a tree first and cast themselves down on to fruit lying below. Normally the objects of attention are described as apples, but occasionally grapes and other soft fruits are mentioned; especially in old accounts from France and Spain where such fruit might be easier for hedgehogs to find. The story is not just a European yarn, but is also told as far away as China. But is it true?

You can certainly demonstrate for yourself that the hedgehog can carry fruit on its back. If you impale a squashy apple on to a patch of spines and jiggle it about, the animal will contract muscles that cause the spines to bristle. This helps to hold the fruit firmly enough to stay in place when the animal walks away. The problem is to understand how a hedgehog could get the fruit stuck there for itself. The old stories say that hedgehogs roll on the apples, but even this, if true, would probably not impale them. Isaac Newton might have supported the suggestion that apples fall from trees with sufficient force to impale themselves, but a hedgehog sitting below is, like Sir Isaac, not expecting random events such as being struck by falling apples. And, in the normal course of relaxed activity or rest, the hedgehog keeps its spines laying flat, not bristling. Falling apples then bounce off, whether they drop on to hedgehogs or distinguished eighteenth-century scientists.

Even supposing a hedgehog did manage to pick up an apple, getting another one would be doubly difficult and making off with a whole back full of booty (as in mediaeval pictures) stretches probability too far.

Medieval drawings of hedgehogs carrying apples

However, the biggest doubts must centre on why the hedgehog would bother at all. When it *needs* to carry things (e.g. nest building material), it uses its mouth not its spines. It has no need to carry fruit at all; it can eat it and any associated slugs and insects right where it lays on the ground. Hedgehogs do not take food back to the nest to feed their young. Nor do they hoard food for the winter as hibernating rodents do: they store their winter energy supply in the form of fat. Of all the hundreds of times I have examined hedgehog winter nests I have never once found anything which might have constituted a hedgehog's larder. If hedgehogs did carry fruit, why don't they similarly make off with bits of bread and milk or roll on worms and slugs to pick them up?

It's a nice story, but it won't do! When the issue was aired on a recent television programme seen by over 12 million viewers, the BBC was not deluged with first-hand twentieth-century observations of fruit-carrying and so we must conclude that the case is 'not proven'.

Hedgehogs in folklore: taking milk from cows

A favourite country tale is that hedgehogs suck milk from cows. This story has a ring of truth about it, albeit a muffled one. Hedgehogs certainly like cow's milk and will rarely ignore a chance to partake of it; but obviously if the cow is standing up the hedgehog is too short to help itself. When cows lie down, their teats are within reach and often ooze milk, droplets of which may spatter the nearby grass advertising availability to any passing hedgehogs. Leakage of milk is most probable when the udder is full after a night's grazing. Thus, hedgehogs are most likely to find milk in the early morning, when the cows are lying down waiting to be called in to the milking shed. It is exactly at this time that the cowhand appears on the scene to fetch the cows and may spot a slurping hedgehog.

So this is a story that *could* be true, up to a point. It's unlikely that a hedgehog could actually suck from a cow. Its mouth does not open wide enough to encompass the average teat and even if it did, the cow would probably react indignantly to the hedgehog's teeth. It is interesting that a veterinary research journal reported a few years ago that teat damage had been observed which was consistent with the peculiar size and shape of hedgehog teeth. Maybe some hedgehogs occasionally push their luck a bit far. Otherwise there seems to be little harm in letting a drop of excess milk end up in a hedgehog's stomach.

Hedgehogs in folklore: proof against snakebite?

It has long been suggested that hedgehogs are immune to the bite of snakes. One major Russian zoologist even went so far as to say that this enables hedgehogs to prey extensively on serpents and that a shortage of snakes in some areas may be a major cause of hedgehog scarcity!

It is true that hedgehogs are resistant to the snake's *bite*, but not its venom. The distinction is important. In Britain, our only poisonous snake is the adder; there are other poisonous species on the Continent but none is very large. In every case the fangs are shorter than a hedgehog's spines. So, when investigators in the past (not me) have set up a gladiatorial contest between hedgehog and snake, they observe the snake striking in a series of futile attacks against the spiny armour of the hedgehog. Not only do the fangs fail to reach the skin underneath and cause any harm, but the bristling spines inflict mortal injury on the snake, which suffers multiple perforations. Moreover, if the hedgehog responds by biting the snake, the snake jerks and the hedgehog rolls up. If it still has a grip on the reptile, the hedgehog will then be rolled up around it, exerting all the force of its rolling up muscles to stretch the snake and force further spines into it. The action is automatic, not deliberate, and very effective (if you are holding a hedgehog and it suddenly rolls up, trapping your fingers inside the spiny ball, you soon get a very uncomfortable insight into the fate of the luckless snake). The result of these conflicts is often death or disablement of the snake, and the hedgehog may follow up its triumph by making a meal of its foe.

Thus far the folk story appears true. However, should the snake manage a lucky strike on the hedgehog's unprotected face or leg, where the skin is quite thin, a dose of venom can be delivered which will make the hedgehog very ill or even kill it in a few hours. More scientific tests on resistance to experimentally injected doses of poison suggest that hedgehogs are more resistant than some other common animals, but hedgehogs are not immune to snake venom.

Under the special circumstances of hibernation, hedgehogs are observed to be extraordinarily resistant to many poisonous substances. They are able to survive massive overdoses of poisons that would kill much larger animals several times over. Hibernating hedgehogs can also survive half an hour in poisonous carbon monoxide gas; they are even abnormally unaffected by ionizing radiation. However, these hardly constitute natural threats in the wild; the hedgehog's surprising ability to cheat death while it is in hibernation is of only academic interest rather than real use in the everyday world. Although it would be true to say that a hibernating hedgehog would not be killed by a snake's bite, this is again purely academic. If the hedgehog was in hibernation, the snake would be too.

Hedgehog research

I am often asked what sort of research is being done on hedgehogs and have to confess that it's very little. Laboratory studies have investigated aspects of breeding and hibernation; some field work has been done to look at various ecological topics (though more has been done in New Zealand and Scandinavia than in Britain). My own studies and those of my students represent a very small effort which barely scratches the surface. For example we have looked at home range, feeding and hibernation in parkland and on a suburban golf course (because working in the dark in open grassy habitats is fairly easy) but these are rather peculiar habitats. We haven't tried yet to tackle even farmland hedgehogs, let alone those that live in woodland; yet their behaviour and activities might be quite different.

The technical problems of working on hedgehogs are very considerable; worse is the difficulty of studying a nocturnal animal when our own lives are geared to daytime work. You can't do both and a few nights out with the hedgehogs plays havoc with your social life, not to mention any other daytime work you are supposed to do.

But the main problem is money. Because the hedgehog is not an endangered species or a serious economic pest, it gets overlooked. Money is directed towards studying other more 'deserving' (though better understood) species. Some of the royalties from the sale of this book will be used to support studies in hedgehogs – so go out and buy another 10 copies! There isn't a lot of research money about these days, but even the smallest study costs an extraordinary amount. In our 4-week investigation of hedgehogs and food bowls, we drove 26 miles a day: over 600 miles in all. The students who did the donkey work each put in 6 hours or more per night (non-stop, no meals or tea breaks), totalling 400+ man-hours. Any kind of reasonable payment soon runs up a big bill, even without counting the cost of equipment, torch batteries, computer time and so on. A full time research assistant of the cheapest kind costs about £5,000 per year without paying for vehicle costs or equipment. Who's going to spend that much on hedgehogs?

There are also several specialized projects that need investigation, but these will require big research grants and will have to wait their turn in the face of competition from other grant-seekers. One such area of study would be an investigation of the energy requirements of hedgehogs, another would look into the role of scent glands in the ecology and behaviour of the hedgehog. There are also a lot of small things that can be investigated even as a hobby by people at home (e.g. marking and behaviour observations, see pp. 77–9). Despite their simplicity these little studies may yield interesting and novel information.

Further reading

Because there has been little research on hedgehogs there's been little to write about. Hence there are few 'popular' books available. Most of the detailed studies of hedgehogs have been published as short papers in scientific journals, so are not easily available to most folk. The following books can be purchased or obtained via a local library, but several are long out of print and unlikely to be found except in secondhand bookshops.

M. Burton, The Hedgehog (André Deutsch, London, 1969)

G.B. Corbet & H.N. Southern, The Handbook of British Mammals (Blackwell, Oxford, 1977)

L. Harrison–Matthews, British Mammals (Collins New Naturalist, London, 1952)

K. Herter, Hedgehogs (Phoenix House, London, 1965)

P. Morris, The Hedgehog (Forest Record No. 77, H.M.S.O., London. 1973)

Information

The 'British Hedgehog Preservation Society', founded by Major Adrian Coles, has been collecting money to help pay for the construction of ramps which allow hedgehogs to escape from cattle grids. The newly formed society also aims to promote reasearch on hedgehogs and issue a Newsletter to friends of the hedgehog. The address is: British Hedgehog Preservation Society, Knowbury House, Knowbury, Shropshire.

The Mammal Society (Harvest House, London Road, Reading RG1 5AS) is a national organization which seeks to promote inter-est in the study of mammals. Membershi includes professional biologists, teacher and also non-biologists with an interest in mammals. A Youth Group caters for th under 18s. The society issues a Newsletter t members 4 times a year, the Journal Mamma Review and has meetings at least twice a year.

The County Naturalist's Trusts (addres from your local library) support and co ordinate wildlife conservation at a loca level. One of them (Northants) even has th hedgehog as its official symbol.

Postscript: slug pellets

The controversy as to whether or not slug pellets are harmful to hedgehogs continues; further unpublished work on the Continent suggests that poisoned slugs may indeed be dangerous to hedgehogs and various manu-facturers are bringing so-called 'safe' slug pellets onto the market. In the UK a product is available which is not a bait to be eaten, but acts by drying up the slime-formin organs of slugs and snails that come into contact with it. It is marketed by Fertosar Products Ltd, 2 Holborn Square, Lowe Tranmere, Birkenhead, Merseyside L4 9HQ. In Germany, the manufacturers of a 'safe' slug pellet are: Celamerck, Postfac 507, Ingelheim, Rhein, W. Germany.

Index